True Christianity:

It May Not Be What You Think

Third Edition

Published by James E. Gibson, Freelance Writer
Lexington, KY

James E. Gibson

True Christianity: It May Not Be What You Think, Third Edition
Copyright © 2017, 2019 by James E. Gibson.
All Rights Reserved. No part of this book may be reproduced or transmitted in any form or by any means without written permission from the copyright owner, James E. Gibson, with the exception of brief quotes that are considered "fair use" under copyright law.

Third Edition published September 9, 2017, with dozens of small corrections/changes made later in September 2017, and numerous additional ones in mid-May 2019 and again later in May 2019. The Second Edition is copyright 2015, and it was originally published September 2, 2015, with numerous small corrections/changes made on September 28, 2015, (expanded and updated from the First Edition with seven additional chapters, updated links, and some corrections/changes). The First Edition is copyright 2014, and it was originally published March 28, 2014, with numerous small corrections/changes made on April 2, June 1, July 18, December 11, and December 30, 2014).

Third Edition International Standard Book Number: 978-0-9988774-1-9
Third Edition Library of Congress Control Number: 2017911950
The book is also available in three ebook forms (for Amazon Kindle, for Barnes & Noble NOOK, and for Kobo).

Second Edition ISBN: 978-0-9915416-4-5
Second Edition LCCN: 2015913718
First Edition ISBN: 978-0-9915416-0-7
First Edition LCCN: 2014903009

Published by James E. Gibson, Freelance Writer
P.O. Box 54868, Lexington, KY 40555-4868
United States of America   Email: jamesegibson@gmail.com

You may contact the author at the address above. He appreciates all comments, questions, suggestions, etc., but he cannot promise to provide a personal reply to everyone.
Hyphens in URLs (even at the end of lines) are part of the URLs.

Table of Contents

Acknowledgments 4
About the Front Cover 4
Miscellaneous Details About Sources 5
Disclaimer 6
Introduction 7
Part I: Defining and Practicing True Christianity 13
   1. True Christianity 13
   2. The Golden Rule 17
   3. Be Truthful Always—Avoid Telling "White Lies" 19
   4. A Positive Attitude, Positive Actions, and Humility Can Lead to Happiness, Joy 23
   5. Ten Guidelines for Living Joyously 27
   6. Prayer 30
   7. How I Became a Christian—And How My Faith Has Evolved ... 35
Part II: Specific Attitudes and Beliefs 39
   8. Jesus as Son of Man 39
   9. The United States as a Christian Nation—Not Really 45
  10. Capitalism, Socialism, Communism, Geography, and God 51
  11. Resurrection from the Dead Is Impossible—Or Is It? 54
  12. Virgin Birth 57
  13. Capital Punishment and Christianity 59
  14. Euthanasia and End-of-Life Issues 63
  15. "Miraculous" Healings and "Speaking in Tongues" 66
  16. Being Pro-Life, the Abortion Issue 71
  17. Creationism and Evolution Can Both Be Right Within Limits 74
  18. Equality of Opportunity, Yes! Same Skills, No! 80

19. Providing City Services to Rural Areas 83
20. What Does It Mean to Honor Your Father and Your Mother? 85
21. Homosexual Rights, Gay Marriage, and Lust (Heterosexual and Homosexual) 91
22. Nonviolent Conflict Resolution 96

Part III: Specific Behaviors 99
23. Better Preventive Care—True Health Care Reform 99
24. A Christian Work Ethic, Unemployment Benefits, and Retirement 107
25. Choosing a Career 110
26. Budgeting 113
27. Sexual Abstinence Until Marriage Is Best 115
28. Choosing Singleness—A Great Option 122
29. Parenting 125
30. Drinking Alcoholic Beverages Socially in Moderation—Risks Outweigh Benefits 128
31. Reducing One's Food Budget (And Other Benefits of a Vegan Diet) 134
32. The "Miracle" of the Digestive System and the Immune System 142
33. Free and Cheap Ways to Have Fun 144
34. Playing Games—Old Fashioned Fun 149
35. Emergency Preparedness Kit Setup and Preparing for a Disaster 153
36. Piercings and Tattoos 159
37. Gambling May Lead to Major Problems 161
38. Neckties: Attractive? Elegant? Actually Unnecessary and Unsafe 165
39. Wearing High Heel Shoes—Definite Health Risks—Any Benefit? 167

40. Is the High School Prom Important? Maybe No 170

Part IV: Relationship Between Christianity and Some Other Things 176

    41. Atheism and Atheist Madalyn Murray O'Hair 176

    42. Agnosticism 182

    43. Religions Other Than Christianity 184

    44. Witchcraft, Kabbalah, Freemasonry, Astrology, and "Magic" ... 189

    45. Hypnotism 196

    46. Mental Illness (Bipolar Disorder, etc.) 200

    47. ESP (Extrasensory Perception) 205

    48. Extraterrestrial Life 207

    49. Truth May Sometimes Seem Stranger Than Fiction 209

    50. God's Magnificent Creation—Huge Cave Along the Kentucky-Virginia Border 219

Part V: Summary 225

    51. Summary/Epilogue 225

Endnotes (Details for Internet Links in the Book) 229

About the Author 238

Order Form and Ordering Information 239

Acknowledgments

The highest righteous power, God, deserves the credit and glory for any good that comes from this book. Without God I could do nothing and indeed would not even exist. My relatives, friends, neighbors, coworkers, and everyone else that I've encountered in my life also deserve great thanks for their help. All have helped me immensely in various ways over the years of my life thus far.

These individuals are too numerous to mention specifically by name. In fact, to help prevent persons from getting undesired publicity, I seldom mention names and specific personal information in the book. However, I love everyone and appreciate the positive roles everyone has played in my life. Thank you all very much!

About the Front Cover

The color white symbolizes purity. White also in a sense contains all colors. The white cover on the book thus symbolizes both the purity that true Christians strive for and the unity of all under God's control.

The seven colored horizontal lines represent all the diversity of God's creation, while also adding color to the cover.

The blue in the book title refers symbolically to the heavens, the sky, and God. The green (in the subtitle and the author's name) symbolizes human greenness, our limited knowledge about God and the immensity of creation.

The purple in the edition number symbolizes the ministry of serving others, the ongoing progress to help produce a better book.

The simple cover that I created (under God's leadership I hope) also saved me the expense of hiring a professional cover designer—and enabled me to create the cover my (God's?) way.

Miscellaneous Details About Sources

All Bible scripture quotations are taken from the King James Version (1611), but please feel free to check the references in any Bible version. All other quotations (from sources other than the author's own previous writings, which are mentioned in the paragraphs below) are either from sources in the public domain or are brief enough to constitute "fair use" under copyright law.

This is the first time that some of the content of *True Christianity: It May Not Be What You Think*, Third Edition, has been published. But most of the content of this book is modified from articles, comments, and/or letters the author wrote that were previously published elsewhere, in addition to being published in the first and/or second edition of the book.

The original publication primarily occurred in articles on two websites that no longer exist: Yahoo! Voices (and its predecessor Associated Content) under the author's name "James Gibson," and Newsvine.com under the username "jameseg" (though the author's homepage/column on Newsvine contained the author's name "James Edwin Gibson" in addition to his username).

In addition to being previously published in some form on one or more of the above websites, some of the book is adapted from material the author wrote that was previously published under his name on other websites, in a newspaper op-ed piece, and in letters to the editor of various publications.

Much has been thought, said, and written about Christianity over the last approximately 2,000 years. And many of the topics covered in this book predate Christianity. If anything I've written inadvertently plagiarizes someone else's words, I apologize. Please notify me, and if I find this to be the case, I will seek to cite the original source or delete the material if it is not fair use.

Disclaimer

All the opinions expressed in this book are those of the author (me, James E. Gibson). They do not reflect the views of any particular Christian denomination or any other organization, nor do they reflect the views of any other individual Christian or nonChristian.

Although I have read the complete Bible in English a few times and many passages (especially in the New Testament) several additional times, I do not claim to be a Bible scholar, and I know no Greek, Hebrew, or Aramaic.

Some events described in the book are based on my personal memories. In such cases, I sought to be accurate and to express my opinions honestly in a relatively positive way; God deserves the credit to the extent that I succeeded. Errors could occur due to my misunderstanding events originally when they happened, faulty personal memory, or errors in my writing.

I love everyone and hope nothing I've written offends anyone.

Introduction

Authentic Christianity seeks to unite rather than to divide. Therefore, *True Christianity: It May Not Be What You Think* in a sense focuses more on helping persons of various faiths (and even atheists and agnostics) overcome problems and unite for the common good of humanity than it does on the traditional doctrines of the Christian faith.

Indeed, I feel that many morals and teachings are universal. As I see it, "true Christianity" (or "authentic Christianity" or "real Christianity") is much different from Christianity as practiced by most self-professed believers and as taught by most denominational churches.

This third edition includes numerous small corrections, changes, and/or updates, hundreds total, that improve the book.

This book is subdivided into five parts. Part I offers a definition of true Christianity and provides basic guidelines for practicing it. Even if you've read (or heard) much of Part I's information previously elsewhere, my simple, straightforward, brief approach may help you apply these guidelines better. Much of it is common sense, but often common sense isn't applied.

Part II deals with specific attitudes and beliefs. Since true Christians (as I see it) can be more conservative than today's conservatives on some issues and more liberal than today's liberals on others, I am confident each group will praise certain chapters (and criticize others as heresy). For example, I urge conservatives to try to read with an open mind my chapter titled "Jesus as Son of Man" that uses quotes from the book of John to demonstrate Jesus' humanity. I urge liberals to be similarly open-minded when reading my strong stance in the chapter titled "Being Pro-Life, the Abortion Issue."

Part III focuses on specific behaviors, things I believe true Christians will do. Some topics covered (diet, sexual abstinence before marriage, and a Christian work ethic) are commonly discussed, but others are so seldom discussed in the context of Christianity that persons may wonder why they were included—at least until they read the chapters.

Part IV deals with how Christianity relates to some other things. Chapter 41 focuses on the personal story of how what atheist Madalyn Murray O'Hair said (and how she said it) affected me when I was an agnostic considering atheism in 1979. Other chapters in this section discuss topics such as hypnotism and ESP, which I feel some use in their practice of what they call "Christianity" to mislead or "fool" believers. This part also discusses other religions, witchcraft, and "magic."

Part V contains the final chapter, which offers a brief summary/epilogue for the book.

During the decades since I changed from an agnostic to a Christian I have visited one or more churches in a variety of denominations (Southern Baptist, nondenominational Christian, Roman Catholic, Assembly of God, Apostolic, United Methodist, Free Methodist, Episcopalian, Lutheran, Presbyterian, Free Will Baptist, independent Baptist, Nazarene, Church of Christ, Jehovah's Witnesses, Church of Jesus Christ of Latter-day Saints, etc.).

In my spare time, I also devoted several hours to reading in two seminary libraries near where I live, but I am neither an ordained minister nor a Bible scholar. My college degrees are in engineering and business—though I took several undergraduate electives in English and some graduate school courses in Communications. I have loved to read and write since childhood. I write this book as a layman sharing in simple language from what I have learned and observed.

By the way, I enjoyed visiting each church congregation I've been to, met many fine people, and my faith evolved and grew from these visits, as well as from my reading in various sources and praying. Still, what I saw and experienced in the churches differed from what I learned from reading prayerfully in the New

Testament about the Christian church. These churches I visited seemed to fall far short of practicing true Christianity. Of course, I also fall far short of achieving perfection in practicing real, authentic, true Christianity. But I seek to progress closer toward it. Furthermore, through God, I feel that I am progressing closer toward practicing true Christianity. I hope this book will help many others to do so, too.

I believe firmly that many young persons (and adults) see the hypocrisy and false doctrines of various "Christian" denominations, congregations, and individuals, then reject Christianity itself. True Christianity is very different from what is apparently taught and practiced in most churches.

I became a Christian by reading a New Testament with an open mind, prayerfully. My faith has evolved over the years—and my faith is still evolving. I don't seek to judge any specific Christian since all Christians (including me) share in the responsibility for the shortcomings of our applications of Christian principles.

A significant part of this book is somewhat autobiographical; even the portions that are not reflect my own views based on my background and experiences. Still, I have sought to present unbiased facts and emphasize basic truths rather than focusing just on my opinions. Of course, what constitutes "fact" and what constitutes "opinion" is subject to change as time goes by and knowledge and wisdom advance.

My hope is that through the guidance of the Holy Spirit I have managed to write in a way that is positive, upbeat, and helpful to a wide variety of people in various ways. Several topics in the book are important. Others are arguably just important to a few—including me.

Some of the incidents described here may seem strange, perhaps even unbelievable, especially my writings in the last few chapters of the book, particularly Chapter 49 (titled "Truth May Sometimes Seem Stranger Than Fiction"). Some chapters are based almost totally on my personal perspective. Others, especially Chapter 30 on alcoholic beverages, include numerous references to other sources.

At the end of the book I provide Endnotes that give more information about all the Internet articles whose URLs are given in the book from the Introduction through the Summary/Epilogue, so readers can (I hope) find the particular articles somewhere even if the URLs printed in the text are no longer active. I believe most of the URLs will remain active for years, though.

In cases where I mention books, I provide the title and enough information about the book in the text that readers can (I hope) find it in a local library, a bookstore, or elsewhere, if they choose to.

Considering this book deals with true Christianity, I cite relatively few scriptures, and in most of those citations I just list the reference rather than quoting it. Readers may feel free to use any Bible version they prefer when checking my scripture citations. When I do quote directly from the Bible I use the King James Version (KJV) of 1611, which is widely available and probably known to most readers in one way or another. In my own daily Bible reading, I frequently use the New International Version (copyright 1973, 1978, 1984 by International Bible Society; published by Zondervan Bible publishers). The New International Version (NIV) is a bit paraphrased but uses simple modern language that is often easier to understand than the KJV. Though I am certainly not a Bible scholar, I have read the entire Bible in English three or four times, including once in the KJV and once in the NIV.

Since I did not become a Christian until adulthood, am not an ordained minister, and am currently a nondenominational Christian who visits various churches rather than belonging to a specific one (though previously I belonged to a Southern Baptist church, then two nondenominational Christian churches), I feel that to some extent I can write as an outsider as well as an insider, from a layman's perspective primarily for other laymen. Also, as a member of the worldwide Christian church, I consider myself a part of each congregation everywhere in a sense.

All human beings everywhere are linked together in some way as part of God's creation. And all Christians everywhere are linked together as part of the worldwide Christian Church. It would be wonderful if we all worked together more effectively as part of God's team to improve our planet. I hope this book in at least a small way helps us progress toward that.

My goal is to be truthful, in a compassionate way, and not to offend others unnecessarily. The reader can be the judge of how well this book achieves that. If readers have any comments, constructive criticism, etc., please feel free to email me at jamesegibson@gmail.com. I will try to answer all emails seeking a reply, but that will depend on the volume, etc.

Parts of the book are very entertaining in my opinion, and I include a few personal anecdotes. However, I dislike the trend for nonfiction books to emphasize entertaining personal anecdotes and hyperbole at the expense of accuracy. To put it bluntly, I think hyperbole is a fancy word for lying and ought to be limited to fiction, rather than be a part of nonfiction books. Believe it or not, even the personal experiences discussed in chapter 49 are factual if my memory is accurate, not hyperbole. I hope the book will to some extent inform, inspire, and entertain you.

Each chapter following this introductory chapter contains two or more "Questions for Reflection and Discussion" at its end. These sometimes provocative questions are designed primarily to encourage deeper thought by individual readers, but they also can help foster better discussions in classes or other group book study situations. In some cases the questions serve as a way to introduce topics I chose not to include in the book for various reasons. Readers certainly can add their own questions to reflect upon and discuss.

Thanks to God for any worthwhile insights contained in this book—for I could do nothing on my own. Thanks to you for reading. Enjoy God's blessings!

Part I: Defining and Practicing True Christianity

Chapter 1: True Christianity

As I see it, true Christianity is much different from the Christian religion that many nonbelievers condemn. Indeed, true Christianity often attracts compliments and praise from nonbelievers, rather than offending them. Below I discuss some basic components of this "true Christianity" in my view.

Loving Service

Loving service is a key aspect of real Christianity. It includes serving others by giving to the poor, helping the sick, and in general caring for one's fellow human beings.

True Christianity includes practicing love for others, even one's enemies, as Jesus and the Apostle Paul both taught, according to the New Testament. If you doubt me, please see Matthew 5:44, Luke 6:27, and Romans 12:20 for scripture references urging persons to demonstrate love for their enemies.

Fellowship

Fun fellowship is also a part of authentic Christianity. This fellowship can take many forms. It is not limited to worship in a church building. In fact some Christians fellowship with other Christians in their family, neighborhood, and workplace and don't regularly attend a particular denominational church in a formal church building. My best fellowship with other Christians comes as I meet and interact with them in daily activities.

Evangelism

Evangelism is also a part of true Christianity. But it is largely evangelism in the sense of answering questions from others who want to know the reasons for the joy Christians have. Real Christianity attracts others and brings questions from them.

By living a Christian life where we are and where we travel to, we spread Christianity by our example, rather than by formal evangelism. Others will see our joy, our compassionate attitude, and our service, then ask us questions about why we are so happy and why we do what we do. This opens an opportunity for evangelism.

Persons often compliment me for being positive and upbeat. I can then explain that God deserves the credit for making me so happy.

Teamwork

Teamwork is a key to success. Rather than a pastor, missionary, deacon, elder, or other Christian leader doing all the work, in a true Christian church each believer is to do an honest day's work as part of the body of Christ. New members may lack the training or skills of those who have been taught well and who benefit from many years of experience, but each can contribute in some way.

This teamwork in service doesn't necessarily mean serving inside a four-walls congregation either. Even the numerous tasks that need done in a given church don't require a lot of hours from every member. Therefore, most Christians do the vast majority of their Christian service outside the church building—in their community and in other communities. This is certainly true of me.

In fact many congregations either write in their weekly bulletins or post somewhere in their church buildings words something like "enter to worship, leave to serve." Worship times in church may be relatively passive for many Christians who are sitting in the pews absorbing insights. Their Christian service comes during the remainder of the week. Serving God (the highest righteous authority) and others can occur anytime, anywhere. I hope church members realize that the blessings gained in worship in church and/or through personal devotional times at home are to be applied in their activities throughout the day and the week.

Rest

Getting adequate rest is part of Christianity, too. Avoid being a workaholic. Indeed, each member of the flock doing his or her own share of the labor makes it go more smoothly.

A Christian working 80 or 100 hours a week will exhaust himself or herself physically, mentally, emotionally, and spiritually. Burnout comes. It is far better to train others to do some things, then work together to experience the blessings that come from completing tasks. Each of us can learn something from any other person and teach any other person something. As each of us do our part, much necessary work can be done, while allowing significant time for rest (and other activities), too.

Summary—and Tolerance for Other Faiths

Some persons refer to Christians as being "born again." This term is accurate in the sense that instead of continuing to live their lives selfishly according to their natural desires, after becoming Christians persons commit to obeying the highest righteous authority, God, and thus commit to seeking what is best: showing love to others and to themselves.

Doing this is somewhat like living a new life. I urge readers to seek to do this. Confess your sins, renounce them, and prayerfully seek to be obedient to God, loving others and yourselves. In simple terms, obeying the highest righteous authority (which I call God) by loving and caring for others and oneself is what true Christianity is all about. Using this definition, even those who do not profess to be Christians can seek to practice true Christianity.

As Romans 2:14 puts it in the King James Version (KJV) of the Bible: "For when the Gentiles, which have not the law, do by nature the things contained in the law, these, having not the law, are a law unto themselves:"—which I think are very wise words from the Apostle Paul's letter to the Romans. Paul was comparing Gentiles to Jews, but I think the parallel applies to others, too.

Yes, some atheists, agnostics, Buddhists, Hindus, Muslims, and followers of other religions may be practicing a form of true Christianity. They may do things Jesus taught and produce the fruit of the Spirit through their words and deeds, even though they don't call themselves Christians. I'm confident some do through the grace of God. If you aren't sure what I meant earlier in this paragraph by the fruit of the Spirit, please see Galatians 5:22, 23 for details.

I am happy to refer to "nonbelievers" who obey God (the highest righteous authority) without even knowing it by the title "honorary true Christians."

The world can and will be a much better place when we have more persons practicing true Christianity or at least coming close to it, whether these practitioners accept the official title Christians or not.

In a sense, a key to practicing true Christianity is to treat others and oneself fairly, to obey the golden rule. In the next chapter, I discuss what the golden rule is—and what it is not.

Chapter 1 Questions for Reflection and Discussion
1. How would you define "true Christianity"?
2. What can you do to serve others better?
3. How can you improve your fellowship with others?
4. What do you think is the key to successful evangelism?
5. What are some things you can do to ensure getting adequate rest, without becoming lazy or inattentive to necessary duties?
6. Do you agree that followers of other faiths (or even agnostics or atheists) can be Christians by practicing a form of Christianity without either acknowledging it themselves or being recognized as Christians by members of mainstream Christian denominations? Why do you agree or disagree?

Chapter 2:
The Golden Rule

The golden rule is a foundation of many religions. It basically states that we are to treat others the way we would like to be treated.

If we all sincerely sought to lovingly apply this one rule, it could make the world a much better place—but applying it isn't easy.

For example, I love peanuts. However, if I give someone a jar of peanuts, as I might like for them to give me one, they might die if they suffer from a severe allergy to peanuts. Even my eating peanuts near them could be fatal to them.

As a second example, I considered it nice to offer someone some spaghetti I had made. If she had accepted, it could have been fatal due to her severe allergy to mushrooms, which the spaghetti sauce contained. I'm glad she knew enough to ask if the spaghetti sauce contained mushrooms.

Similarly, I often enjoy privacy. I might consider obeying the golden rule to include giving my neighbors privacy. If my neighbors enjoy fellowship, they might consider obeying the golden rule to require visiting me regularly and enjoying lengthy conversations about our daily activities.

Each individual is different. Applying the golden rule properly requires: (1) finding out what makes others happy, (2) seeking to do that within reasonable limits, and (3) others seeking to find out what makes us happy and doing it within reasonable limits.

Fortunately, when we treat others well, they frequently do try to reciprocate. Still, successfully following the three steps above may require some compromises and/or associating mainly with those who most resemble us in views and interests. It also includes learning better how to recognize when others are in need and how to help them—as we would like them to help us when necessary.

It is also important to determine not to intentionally take advantage of anyone—just as we don't want others to take advantage of us (or anyone else). Obeying the golden rule leads to everyone doing his or her fair share.

Treating everyone fairly, rejoicing with others when they succeed, ministering to them in their hurts, and each of us benefiting from the bonds of friendship that develop, are admirable goals to seek after.

But following the golden rule isn't easy. I almost always fall short in my attempts, so I don't feel qualified to give expert advice on how to best adhere to it. Obeying the golden rule does often seem to work "miracles" though—on the occasions when I do succeed in practicing the golden rule along the guidelines listed in this chapter, through the grace of God.

I can see why the golden rule is such an important part of so many religions and laws in one way or another. I love the golden rule. Its principles are foundational to parts of some of the following chapters in this book, including the next chapter on being truthful always.

Chapter 2 Questions for Reflection and Discussion
1. How would you answer someone who says the golden rule is simple?
2. What (if anything) will you do to come closer to practicing the golden rule?
3. How reasonable do you think it is to expect individuals to practice the golden rule?

Chapter 3:
Be Truthful Always—Avoid Telling "White Lies"

A major key to making this world a much better place is for everyone to seek to always do the right thing. I believe this includes seeking to always be truthful—in a loving way.

I like for others to always be truthful with me. And, I try to always be truthful myself.

The Apostle Paul urged persons to be ". . . speaking the truth in love . . ."(Ephesians 4:15, King James Version). Great advice!

Is lying always wrong? Yes, I think so.

Don't Lie to Children

When I was a child, my mom told me I could receive gifts from the Easter Bunny, the Tooth Fairy, and Santa Claus. I had doubts about their existence even at a young age. But I resisted questioning my beliefs because mom's words to me indicated a correlation between lack of faith and not receiving certain gifts. This created a form of dishonesty in a sense for a period, as I pretended to believe or at least didn't try to question my belief—I didn't want to miss out on the goodies. To my great pleasure, the Easter baskets and Christmas gifts continued long after my faith in the live existence of the Easter Bunny and Santa Claus ended.

I think it would be better for children to be told the truth. Parents can leave coins under the pillows of children who lose teeth, provide kids Easter baskets, and give gifts to their sons and daughters at Christmas. But don't lie about the source of the gifts.

It is wrong to set a precedent for lying. For example, instead of telling lies about Santa Claus, moms and dads can read to their children about the possibly true story regarding the Bishop of Myra, who came to be called Saint Nicholas. He reportedly performed some "miracles," including at least a few that helped children.

Kids and adults can also enjoy the fictional tales about Santa Claus—while acknowledging they are fiction. If persons ask me if I believe in Santa Claus, I can honestly reply no, but that I do believe in Saint Nicholas.

How to Be Truthful

Being truthful doesn't mean always telling everyone everything. There are some things better left unspoken. On such topics, one can simply say, "I prefer not to express an opinion on that," or "I think it is better not to answer that," or "I promised not to say," or something similar.

But be truthful. If one is polite and persistent, respect will be earned from many for this. I found this to be true personally when individuals trusted me to give them an honest opinion on something or trusted me to keep personal information they disclosed to me secret.

Are "white lies" ever acceptable? No, I don't think so. Being truthful in a loving way is always superior to telling a so-called "white lie" in my view. Often people recognize the lie or learn about it later, anyway.

Don't always provide a detailed answer though. Frequently a brief truthful answer is better than a lengthy, detailed one. Young children often need less information than older children do. Casual acquaintances need fewer details about some personal matters than close friends or relatives. Also, sometimes a short answer is necessary due to limited time.

Lying by the Government and the Religious Is Unacceptable

Certain actions of the CIA, NSA, United States military forces, etc., may need to be kept secret. Still, even those organizations often misuse secrecy to cover up abuses and mistakes, in my opinion as an outsider. Accountability of some type needs to accompany secrecy. Furthermore, as basically a pacifist, I support more openness, better education, and more humanitarian aid, as alternatives to secretive military operations.

The words of Jesus and Paul in the New Testament instruct us to love our enemies, not to conduct covert operations against them.

Even intelligence agencies' employees ought not tell lies in my opinion. Their employees can refuse to answer questions, but so-called "white lies" by anyone are still lies and unnecessary.

It may be even worse when religious leaders lie. Lying is against the teachings of many religions. Christians, Muslims, Jews, and followers of many other faiths are supposed to be truthful as part of their obedience to God.

If followers of all faiths sought to be truthful and to seek the truth, maybe one day the divisiveness due to religious conflict would end. After all, when contradictions between faiths exist, only one at most can be right.

It would be great if we all found and followed the true faith—whatever it is. And I hope this book helps us progress toward that, at least in a small way.

Am I Always Truthful?

Do I always tell the truth? I try very hard to always be truthful—but I fail. Perhaps no one is ever 100% truthful. Being truthful always is very difficult.

However, I know from experience that the times I have not been truthful seem to have frequently caused negative consequences. Therefore, I intend to try even harder to be 100% truthful in the future. I urge others to seek to always be truthful as well.

If we all seek to humbly be truthful about our mistakes and to present the truth in a positive, loving way, I'm confident we will be blessed. Indeed, a positive attitude and humility are two keys to success. I discuss them in the next chapter.

Chapter 3 Questions for Reflection and Discussion

1. How realistic is it to be truthful always?
2. Do you agree that trying to always be truthful to children is appropriate? Why or why not?

3. Do you think lying by the government or secret organizations is always wrong? Why or why not?
4. Do you feel that lying by church leaders is common? If so, what do you think should be done about it?

Chapter 4:
A Positive Attitude, Positive Actions, and Humility Can Lead to Happiness, Joy

People can be happy and joyful despite trying circumstances or be sad despite experiencing what seem like joyous occasions. A key difference is how people react to events. Also, it is amazing the way little things can make a big difference in our degree of happiness.

What Works

Simple things can make people happy. I noticed that on days when I wore a particular t-shirt with a colorful rainbow and the name of the city I live in on it, people I met seemed to smile at me more and be friendlier toward me. Some specifically complimented me on the shirt. When I wore other shirts that were a dull, drab color, people were not quite as nice.

Seeing my brightly colored shirt apparently made people happier. Their reactions made me happier, too. The t-shirt wasn't that expensive, either.

Little things like changing one's shirt can make a big difference, but I'm not urging you to go out and buy a colorful new t-shirt. Try smiling more. It costs nothing and can have similar effects. I enjoy smiling at others; they usually smile back at me. I think this makes each of us happier.

Furthermore, when I listen in an empathetic or sympathetic way to others with problems, they appreciate it. When I congratulate people on their achievements, the joy is contagious. When I help others, they frequently reciprocate or at least thank me for it. In fact, at least a few have repaid me well over and above what I did for them.

Volunteering to help others helps the person volunteering, too. Volunteering often blesses us more than we (through God) bless the organization or individual(s) we are helping. Doing nice things makes us and others happy.

Even if I just devote a few minutes to picking up litter in my neighborhood, it gives me exercise, fresh air, maybe a chance to talk to a few neighbors or passersby, possibly an opportunity to pet a friendly dog or two, and gives me a good feeling inside.

Try not to help out of selfish motives, though. Don't seek public recognition. Often the biggest joy comes from anonymously helping someone in ways no one else knows about. Yes, helping another person is a reward in itself.

When we do good things we make good things happen. We make ourselves and others happy—in a way that has positive consequences in the future, too.

Truly caring about others and helping them enables us to enjoy life more, but balance is important, too. Be willing to say "no" politely, persistently, and firmly to unreasonable requests. Happiness and joy don't typically come from working 80 or 100 hours a week regularly.

Nor does properly serving others include doing things for them that they can do better themselves. Indeed, my friends often appreciate it more when I show them how to do something themselves than they do when I do it for them. Similarly, I love it when they aid me by showing me how to do something myself.

Relax and Enjoy Our Blessings

In addition to helping each other, we need to relax and fellowship with each other. Taking time to relax and enjoy simple pleasures is part of what makes one blissful.

I enjoy taking nature hikes, enjoying the awesome wonder of God's creation. My leisure activities also include taking bicycle rides, playing board and card games, reading a wide variety of things, attending seminars and lectures, and numerous other things. Even washing dishes or doing other duties around my apartment while listening to an entertaining or informative radio broadcast (or meditating) is relaxing fun.

Fellowshipping and laughing with others brings joy whether playing games, attending sporting events, enjoying informal get-togethers with friends, or participating in various other social events. As a child, it thrilled me just to sit and listen to older relatives describe events from their childhoods.

I can be joyous alone with God. Often, though, fellowshipping and laughing with others brings greater joy.

Humbly Crediting Others, Laughing at Oneself, and Keeping a Positive Attitude Help Create Happiness

This writer is blessed to live a joyous life, but I do not deserve the credit for my joy. As a Christian, I know that my immeasurable blessings come from God and others.

In my personal life, when I took excessive personal pride in an accomplishment, it seemed something negative followed. In contrast, when I humbly acknowledged that the credit belonged to God and others, I received blessings. Being willing to give credit to God and others when one succeeds is important.

Humility is an important attribute well worth striving for. Being humble is difficult for those of us who are normal. It is probably much harder for successful people to be humble, but one reason that they are successful is likely their efforts to humbly give credit when it is due. Benjamin Franklin wrote in his autobiography, *The Autobiography of Benjamin Franklin*, about the difficulty of overcoming pride. He noted that even if "I had completely overcome it, I should probably be *proud* of my humility." I commend Franklin for humbly writing those wise words—and for his numerous other accomplishments.

Acknowledge mistakes, too. Even occasions when we make mistakes can be happy ones. Sometimes I enjoy laughing at myself. I remember one day years ago laughing because I wore two dark blue socks that didn't match. On another day years ago, I somewhat absentmindedly felt in my pants pocket, and wondered where my keys were, since they weren't in the pocket I normally kept them in—until I realized that they were in my other hand. We all make "dumb" mistakes sometimes. It's good to laugh at our own mistakes. Our laughter helps others relax and laugh with us.

Being a positive thinker who looks at the bright side of things is also a key to succeeding at achieving joyful happiness. Perhaps the best and most famous book on the importance of a positive attitude and how to attain it is Norman Vincent Peale's classic from the 1950s, *The Power of Positive Thinking*. In addition to selling millions of copies and helping improve many lives directly over the years (including mine), this book has provided inspiration for a lot of writers (including me). Though Peale's book focuses on establishing and maintaining a positive attitude through Christian behavior, much of the book applies just as well to those of other faiths (or of no faith). I recommend it highly.

The writings of Peale and others have helped numerous persons (including me) to experience joyous living. This writer owes a debt of gratitude to these writings (as well as to relatives, friends, others, and the Holy Spirit) for the blessings I have received. These blessings have positively influenced my thoughts and actions; I hope that in some way this chapter does the same for you.

I am blessed immeasurably and hope you are, too. Let's all enjoy our blessings! And, in the next chapter, I provide ten guidelines that can help us enjoy our blessings.

Chapter 4 Questions for Reflection and Discussion
1. What simple things can you do to make others happier?
2. Are you willing to acknowledge mistakes, learn from them, and possibly laugh about them, or do you try to cover them up? Why?
3. What are some simple activities or simple pleasures that you can easily engage in to make yourself happier?
4. Do you have a positive attitude? If not, what steps do you think you can take to attain a more positive attitude?

Chapter 5:
Ten Guidelines for Living Joyously

(Very loosely adapted from Exodus 20:1–17, King James Version.)

Sunday School classes for children often post the Ten Commandments and urge children to memorize and follow them. Intentions are good and often good effects result.

Personally, though, I sometimes got a negative connotation from the "Thou shalt nots" in the King James Version of the Ten Commandments posted in many churches (and elsewhere). As a New Testament Christian, I prefer to focus on the love for God and others that Jesus and Paul emphasized in the New Testament. Therefore, I prefer to focus on the positive things that we can and ought to do to enjoy ourselves (and to benefit ourselves and others), rather than "Thou shalt nots."

Some years ago, I wrote my own version of the Ten Commandments that focused more on positive concepts. Below is my list of ten guidelines for joyous living, which is revised slightly from a version I finished on March 8, 2006. It is based very loosely upon Exodus 20:1–17 in the King James Version of the Bible.

1. Do the right thing always (always put God's perfect will first).
2. Worship and follow only the highest righteous authority, God (worship truth, not falsehood).
3. Esteem God's name (never blame God for evil or urge God to do evil).
4. Reserve one day weekly to worship, pray/meditate, fellowship, and rest from one's regular work.
5. Honor one's parents; treat them well; obey them unless it means disobeying God. In Chapter 20 I provide much more detail about this and discuss a personal experience I had as a child.

6. Love all people (don't murder anyone or be excessively angry with anyone).
7. If married, be loyal sexually to one's spouse; if single, enjoy nonsexual friendships.
8. Work honestly for one's needs; if unable to work, seek help; don't steal.
9. Be truthful always; always speak the truth in a loving way.
10. Be content with what one acquires honestly; avoid being jealous of others.

I think following the above ten guidelines is a good way to experience peace, joy, and happiness.

Even secular persons might appreciate and seek to follow most of these ten guidelines. Indeed, if they substitute "highest righteous authority" for God, they might sincerely seek to obey them all.

Of course, from a practical point of view, none of us can ever follow all ten of these guidelines perfectly (either as I've written them or as they are recorded in Exodus). But the closer we come to doing so, the more joy and fulfillment we can attain, in my humble opinion.

As I see it, a key to coming closer to following these ten guidelines is to prayerfully seek guidance on how to do so from the highest righteous authority, God. In the next chapter, I discuss prayer.

Chapter 5 Questions for Reflection and Discussion
1. Is it better to rephrase the Ten Commandments in positive terms? Why?
2. Can the ten rules be used by nonChristians (and nonJews) without their accepting Christianity (or Judaism) formally? Why?

3. Is it blasphemy to substitute "highest righteous authority" for God when witnessing to nonbelievers or is it an effective evangelistic tool? Why?

Chapter 6:
Prayer

Studies on Prayer

It is hard to scientifically study prayer because it is impossible to create a control group that is definitely not prayed for. For example, if I pray for God's perfect will in all things, I am praying for everyone. Furthermore, I am confident that any individual in a control group would be prayed for by some friend, relative, coworker, medical professional, minister, or someone else. He or she might even pray for himself or herself.

Despite this difficulty, numerous scientific studies have been done on prayer, with some studies indicating it works and others indicating it doesn't. You can find many articles about these studies on the Internet.

Personally, I am confident prayer works. The reason: I have experienced several answers to specific prayers. I provide two examples of these answered prayers later in this chapter.

Perspective as a Former Agnostic Turned Christian

I am a Christian now, but I used to be an agnostic. Even during the years when I was an agnostic, I said a daily evening prayer to God. One reason was that since I didn't know whether or not God existed, I felt it better to play it safe by speaking daily to God. Second, it made me feel good. I enjoyed thanking God for the blessings I received daily—and on occasion praying for certain things. On the rare days when I actually took the time to try to enumerate several specific blessings I received that day, it made me feel wonderful and helped me appreciate just how fortunate I was. Also, asking God for answer to prayer often made me feel relaxed about things of concern.

I first began my regular evening prayers when I was in elementary school after staying overnight with a friend of mine. That night my friend's dad came into the room and had my friend say his prayers out loud to him before we went to sleep. I enjoyed listening to that and soon afterward began saying an evening prayer each night myself, though I said mine silently to God directly.

Answers came to my prayers sometimes, too, even though I was an agnostic. However, other times, the prayers did not seem to be answered, which I attributed to possibly being due to my agnosticism, some sin in my life, the possible nonexistence of God, or some other factor such as that the answer came and I did not recognize it.

I now enjoy both a morning and evening prayer time, and I seek to be prayerfully receptive to the Holy Spirit's leading throughout the day.

I am confident that I receive guidance in answer to my prayers. Admittedly, there is no scientific way to determine whether the guidance comes from God, my own inner thought processes, or signals relayed from others through some form of ESP much as telephones relay words back and forth between humans. For all I know, the answers to prayer may come via advanced communications from highly intelligent extraterrestrial life forms that for lack of a better word might be called "God" or "angels" by humans.

Although I can't provide scientific evidence to demonstrate how prayer works, I have experienced enough answered prayers to convince me that something in some way can and does often (always?) answer prayers. Until/unless proven otherwise, I choose to call this higher power God and to believe God answers all prayers in one way or another.

One verse that Christians might do well to keep in mind is James 5:16, which states ". . . . The effectual fervent prayer of a righteous man availeth much." (KJV) If we conscientiously seek to confess all our sins, live righteously, and pray for guidance when we don't know what to do, I am confident that we are blessed. I am convinced that prayer works.

I do caution that it is important when praying to seek to ensure that the inner voice one may hear in answer is truly the Holy Spirit, rather than a false teaching. Also, test the accuracy of words spoken aloud by others who claim to have heard God speak to them in answer to prayer. Guidance from the Holy Spirit will help you make a situation better; it will not instruct you to commit a crime, lie, or do some other harmful thing.

Examples of Answered Prayers

Although I personally have experienced many things that I consider answers to prayer, I realize it is not easy to convince others that such things were answers to prayer. Even if I provided a huge list, you might attribute the answers to something other than prayer—or accuse me of lying. So, to save space, I will cite just two examples of what I consider answered prayers.

The first example comes from my college years. When I was in college, a roommate often showered and blow dried his hair early in the morning, waking me up. I usually tolerated it good naturedly, since I typically went right back to sleep soon afterward and slept until either I awakened more normally or my alarm clock went off, and he was a fabulous roommate. One morning, however, I prayed something like, "God, if it be your will, please shut off that blow dryer." Very soon afterward, the blow dryer stopped operating. A few minutes later my roommate came in, shook me softly, and apologized for getting me up, but said his blow dryer had quit working and asked to borrow mine. God (or some unidentified force) certainly stopped that blow dryer.

My roommate coming in to disturb me a few minutes after the blow dryer quit (asking to borrow mine) may have been justice served to me for a somewhat selfish prayer. But if I remember correctly, on that day I didn't even own a blow dryer yet, since at that time I let my hair dry naturally after washing it, so his hair remained wet a while longer that day.

A second example of answered prayer occurred one day several years ago when I was shopping in a supermarket. I saw a baby left alone in a shopping cart by a lady who was probably the child's mother, while the woman went to get some item(s) in a nearby aisle of the store. The baby began moving around in the shopping cart's child seat, then suddenly climbed up and fell out, while the woman was several feet away and didn't see. I was too far away to run and catch the baby. I prayed. I prayed hard. The baby seemed to perform a triple somersault in the air before landing uninjured on its feet, even though it appeared too young to even walk. The startled woman returned to the cart unsure how the baby fell or landed uninjured. I considered it a "miracle" in answer to prayer.

In addition to the above two stories, there are numerous other apparent answers to prayer I have experienced. Some of the unusual events I discuss in Chapter 49 may also involve a form of prayer. Yes, I firmly believe in the power of prayers and feel it is very important to seek to utter them according to God's will, rather than selfishly.

Even Atheists Can "Pray"

In my humble opinion, even atheists can regularly take time to list ways they've been blessed, list areas they can improve in, and enumerate specific ideas on how to improve, then quietly meditate on the list. They can even close their eyes and meditate or reflect without listing anything to meditate on. If insights come (as I think they will), atheists can attribute them to whatever they desire. These atheists might even become believers in God—or at least believe in some type of extrasensory perception (ESP). I discuss ESP in chapter 47.

Whether one calls it prayer, meditation, or just taking time for inner reflection, I think setting aside time each morning and evening for some form of "prayerful" activity is a valuable thing. Take time to think about the previous day's blessings and how changes can be made to make the next day even better. Trying to remain in a prayerful frame of mind throughout the day is even better.

Genuine faith in that higher power I call God and genuine commitment to obey righteous guidance when it comes make the process much more effective in my opinion as a Christian. I sincerely believe prayer is the greatest power on Earth available to human beings.

As stated earlier, I did not always have faith in God or in prayer. In the next chapter, I discuss how I changed from an agnostic to a Christian through open-minded, prayerful Bible study—and how my faith has evolved.

Chapter 6 Questions for Reflection and Discussion
1. Do you agree that scientific study of prayer is extremely difficult due to not being able to create a control group that is not prayed for? Why?
2. Do you think that the two examples of answered prayer provided in the chapter are truly answers to prayer? Why or why not?
3. Could some answered prayers be attributed to ESP or some other unknown power(s)? If so, would that weaken or potentially strengthen faith in a higher power, God?
4. What would you suggest doing to "prove" that an event is an answer to prayer?

Chapter 7:
How I Became a Christian—And How My Faith Has Evolved

Even before I became a Christian, most of my closest friends were Christians of one denomination or another. Still, I remained an agnostic.

Perhaps the key step in my progressing toward becoming a Christian occurred during the Fall 1979 semester at the University of Kentucky. Gideons were handing out free New Testaments on campus.

A Gideon offered me one, but I told him I already had one somewhere. He asked me if I knew where it was. I replied no. He said something like, "here, take another one." And as he placed it in my hand, he added, "And this time, read it." I told him I would.

I didn't want to be a liar. In my opinion no one always tells the truth, but I did try hard to always be truthful and still do. I feel being truthful is the right thing to do. So not long after promising him to read it—perhaps a few days or a few weeks later—I began reading the Gideon New Testament.

I read it prayerfully with an open mind, beginning with Matthew Chapter 1. One evening when I was reading somewhere in the book of Mark, I felt convinced firmly that there was a God and Christianity was the true religion.

I prayed a sinner's prayer of confession, repentance, and acceptance of God/Christ as my Savior on October 18, 1979 and then signed the Gideon New Testament on the inside back cover where a spot was left blank for new believers to sign.

However, I did not start attending church. I had not been in church since I was a young boy, felt uncomfortable visiting on my own, and my roommate did not attend a church. Furthermore, no one invited me to attend church with them for a long time—which was a bit surprising, since in previous years I'd received multiple invitations.

Furthermore, as I continued reading prayerfully with an open mind in the Gideon New Testament (and later in a Bible given to me as a child by mom and dad, which I brought from my mom and dad's house on a visit there), I began to question my faith.

I read things which didn't seem to make sense, including many apparent contradictions in the Bible. My faith wavered, but I continued to read.

The next year my roommate was a Christian. He invited me at least a few times to go to church with him. I turned him down for some reason. Then, finally, I decided that the next time he asked, I would attend church with him. However, surprisingly, he did not invite me again for a very long time. When he finally did, I said yes.

I began attending church regularly with him at the Southern Baptist Church he attended. My roommate didn't attend Sunday School class there, though he said he was active in Sunday School in the church he attended in his hometown—he went home many weekends. After I expressed interest in attending Sunday School to him, however, he mentioned one of our friends in the dorm who did regularly attend Sunday School class at the same Southern Baptist Church. I began attending Sunday School with this other friend. I later began attending Sunday evening services, also.

I continued attending church there. One night during the summer of 1982 I lay awake in bed thinking I needed to make a personal profession of faith and be baptized. I was awake much of that night praying and thinking about it—until I finally committed to do so.

I prayed about when to make the public profession of faith; I wanted to wait until the end of the summer when my friends who didn't attend summer school would be back. I seemed to get an answer stating that was okay. Early in the fall semester that year, in September 1982, I decided to make my public profession of faith. Before leaving for church one Sunday morning, I prayed that God would give me a sign that it was the right day to make my public profession of faith. Perhaps I would have made a public profession of faith that day even if I hadn't gotten a sign. I got a sign, though. That Sunday morning I saw in the church bulletin that they were having a morning baptism; usually they did church baptisms during the evening service. At the close of the morning service, I walked down the aisle and made my public profession of faith. I was baptized at the next scheduled baptism service after that Sunday, which was in October 1982.

Some years later, I moved to another town and transferred my membership to a nondenominational Christian church. After moving to another town, I moved my membership to another nondenominational Christian church. After prayerful consideration, I felt led to withdraw my membership from there and just become a nondenominational Christian, not affiliated with any particular local congregation—though I continued to primarily attend that particular church while I lived in that town and still considered myself linked to them as a member of the worldwide Christian church.

Now, several years later, I remain a Christian, but my faith and views have evolved much over the years. I am a much more ecumenical Christian now than when I joined that Baptist church in 1982. My progress toward practicing true Christianity is still ongoing, too. It is a lifelong process. My views continue to change.

One of the changes is that I typically do not take communion in churches now. Though I greatly appreciate the symbolic importance of partaking of the bread and of the fruit of the vine as a remembrance and as a commitment to make our bodies living sacrifices for God, I feel that the actual eating and drinking is a denominational ritual different from the meal that the disciples shared. More important, eating and drinking with unwashed hands among perhaps a crowd of people whose hands enter the bread vessel offers an opportunity for the spread of disease. Of course, if we pray about it, I am confident that our immune system could protect us if we ate dirt off the floor, but I think it is best not to tempt God by handling the bread with unwashed hands.

Another of the changes over the years is in my views about the Trinity. I discuss my current views on the Trinity in the next chapter, which deals with Jesus' humanity. That chapter also begins Part II of the book, where I focus on specific attitudes and beliefs of true Christians.

Chapter 7 Questions for Reflection and Discussion
1. If you are a Christian, what were the keys to your becoming one?
2. How easy do you think it is to become a Christian by reading the New Testament with an open mind?
3. Do you think it is possible to be an active Christian without being a member of a particular church congregation or even regularly attending church? Why or why not?

This chapter concludes Part I. Before moving on to Part II, please take time to briefly review Part I. The questions below may help.
1. How has your understanding of true Christianity and how to practice it changed after reading these chapters?
2. Do you see how following the golden rule, being truthful in a loving way, having a positive attitude, following basic rules like the ten guidelines in chapter 5, and praying (as well as meditating) can help one come much closer to living an authentic Christian life? Do you agree with the way these topics are presented in the book? Why or why not?

Part II: Specific Attitudes and Beliefs

Chapter 8:
Jesus as Son of Man

Jesus accomplished many great "miracles" according to the New Testament gospels. But I believe Jesus could have done all that without being God, just by being an obedient child of God.

Many Christians consider it blasphemy to imply that Jesus was only a man. Fellow Christians, please read this chapter before accusing this writer of heresy. The word Trinity is not in the Bible. Furthermore, numerous Bible scriptures indicate that Jesus was only a human being rather than being God.

When I was in elementary school one of the boys I played with told me that his dad said that the relationship between Jesus and God was similar to the relationship between Saint Nicholas and Santa Claus. I think the boy said that Jesus was a great man, as was Saint Nicholas, but that the idea that Jesus was God was fictional, as were the tales we typically read about Santa Claus. I think that comparison has a significant amount of truth in it.

It is sad that disputes continue over whether or not Jesus was God. Fortunately, the more time Christians devote to loving and caring for others, the less time is wasted in divisive debates.

Let's make the world a better place by helping others. Let's follow Paul's advice in II Timothy 2:14 to ". . . strive not about words to no profit. . ." (KJV).

Unity and the Trinity

The issue of the Trinity is one of the biggest obstacles to accepting Christianity for a lot of nonbelievers, including many in other major monotheistic religions, such as Islam and Judaism. Even a few Christian denominations (such as Jehovah's Witnesses and Mormons) do not accept the doctrine of the Trinity.

Personally, I became a Christian as an adult by reading the New Testament prayerfully with an open mind. During my reading, I saw no mention of the Trinity. Even after reading the entire New Testament, I did not understand how Jesus could be God.

If we acquire a better understanding of what the Bible says, maybe we can then better help unite Christians and become more effective in witnessing to nonbelievers. I think the Bible clearly demonstrates Jesus' humanity.

Who knows? If Jesus had more closely followed his own instructions to love even one's enemies, instead of turning over tables in the temple and driving out the buyers and sellers, he might have experienced a longer ministry. (See Mark 11:15–16, Matthew 21:12, and Luke 19:45 for this story). Even if Jesus' indignation was justified, I believe it could have been exhibited more effectively. That violent action was a key factor in the series of events that led to his crucifixion soon afterward, in my opinion.

I cited the above story from the three synoptic gospels, however John 2:13–15 contains a similar description. John's gospel is probably the book used most often by Christians who seek to "prove" the truth of the Trinity. To help individuals appreciate how even Christians can reject the divinity of Jesus, I will discuss several quotes from the book of John. Many consider John to be the greatest book in the Bible.

Analyzing Some Quotes from the Book of John

In the book of John and the other gospels, numerous references are made to Jesus praying. I never understood why Christians considered Jesus God if Jesus needed to pray.

I do not believe God needs to pray. If God did pray, whom would God pray to? Yet, Jesus prayed regularly. Thus, rather than being God, Jesus was a man, God's son, who prayed to God frequently. John 17 cites one of Jesus' many prayers. John 17:3 states, "And this is life eternal, that they might know thee the only true God, and Jesus Christ, whom thou hast sent." (KJV) Therefore, Jesus was "sent" by God rather than being God.

Also, instead of calling himself God, Jesus referred to himself as "Son of man" (KJV). He did this numerous times in John and the other gospels. Of course, this does not mean he is not also a "Son of God," since the two terms are not mutually exclusive. In fact, God is the creator of us all and in a sense the Father of us all. As John 1:12 states, all believers receive ". . . power to become the sons of God . . . ." (KJV) Therefore, we Christians are all sons of God. A major difference exists, however, between being a "son of God" and being God. And John 3:16 apparently quotes Jesus as stating that he is God's son, rather than being God.

John details many "miracles" Jesus performed: raising the dead, healing the sick, feeding multitudes with very limited food, etc. Jesus did not claim to do these on his own, though. Instead, Jesus credited God his Father. Jesus stated clearly that he could do nothing were it not for God his Father, stating in John 5:19 ". . . The Son can do nothing of himself . . ." (KJV)

Jesus makes it even clearer that he is a man and not God in John 8:40, which states, "But now ye seek to kill me, a man that hath told you the truth, which I have heard of God . . ." (KJV) Jesus is only a man telling the truth about God—though I might nominate Jesus as the most influential man who ever lived, the man most obedient to God.

After John reports about Jesus being crucified and resurrected, John states in John 20:17 that Jesus told Mary to ". . . go to my brethren, and say unto them, I ascend unto my Father, and your Father; and *to* my God, and your God." (KJV) Thus, he is not calling himself God, stating instead that he is going to God.

Even though Jesus was not God, as a righteous man seeking to obey God, a son of God, Jesus could pray to God his Father and receive guidance through the Holy Spirit. Therefore, Jesus in a sense relayed the words of God his Father and spoke for

God on many occasions. Therefore, Jesus says in John 14:9 ". . . he that hath seen me hath seen the Father . . ." (KJV) So though Jesus was not God, in a sense those who saw and heard Jesus were often seeing and hearing God, as the Holy Spirit directed Jesus' thoughts, words, and actions. In that sense, Jesus was one with God.

In John 12:49, John records Jesus as stating clearly that God directed his words, when Jesus is quoted as stating: "For I have not spoken of myself; but the Father which sent me, he gave me a commandment, what I should say, and what I should speak." (KJV)

It is important to point out as this discussion about John ends that it is always dangerous to quote scripture, because it is very easy to take verses out of context to mislead people. Also, for unbelievers the Bible is not a credible source, so what the Bible says may be irrelevant to them. My purpose in using the quotes I cited from John was to demonstrate that the concept of Jesus being only a man rather than being God is well supported in scripture.

Persons who seek to use John or other gospels to "prove" Jesus' divinity seem in this writer's opinion to be only citing a few select scriptures out of context, in contrast to the numerous scriptures that refer to Jesus' humanity. Perhaps 70 or 80 or more times in the KJV Jesus apparently calls himself "Son of man," in addition to other references to himself as "Son" or "Son of God." Does Jesus even once call himself God?

Closing Thoughts on This and Recommendations

Fellow Christians, please consider what John states on the issue rather than being too dogmatic in support of the doctrine of the Trinity. The book of John provides much evidence to oppose the idea of Jesus being God. You can find lots of additional evidence in the other gospels, as well as in the other books of the Bible—if you take the time to do so.

I hope this chapter has helped persons who believe in the Trinity to rethink their beliefs or at least appreciate how other

Christians can believe differently. Maybe this chapter can also help Christians interact more effectively with Muslims, Jews, and others who accept monotheism, but cannot comprehend the Trinity.

Even more important, if we Christians focus on various areas of ministry to others such as feeding the poor, caring for the disabled, helping widows and orphans, and doing other good deeds, persons will respect us and have a positive view about our faith. They will love us more for our actions than for our words.

Our acts of service then present opportunities to share the gospel. Still, we must be sure to do so in a loving way that unites the faith on its common beliefs, rather than teaching a divisive doctrine to potential new believers that may lead them to either reject the faith or to unfairly condemn those of other denominations and faiths.

Please, let's demonstrate love for all as Jesus taught. Remember, Jesus is recorded as commanding his followers to "Love your enemies" in part of Matthew 5:44 and Luke 6:27 (both KJV). By demonstrating compassionate love we can attain joy and success that lead others to ask the source of our fulfillment.

I find this to be true. People regularly compliment me on being so happy and ask why I am so happy. Then I can witness in love about the gospel.

I know, love, and respect many Christians who espouse strong beliefs in the Trinity. It is even possible (despite my disbelief) that Jesus really is God through some miracle of God.

But, as we spread the gospel, let's all seek to avoid needless controversies over the doctrine of the Trinity. Let's avoid stating that the Trinity is Biblical, when the Bible doesn't mention it even once. Instead, let's use God's words to build up others! When we do, we will enjoy God's blessings!

In addition to the Trinity, another source of divisiveness (in the United States at least) is the conflict over whether or not the United States was established as a Christian nation. I discuss this issue in the next chapter.

Chapter 8 Questions for Reflection and Discussion
1. Do you agree that the book of John (and the rest of the New Testament) supports Jesus being a man, a child of God, not God? Why or why not?
2. Do you think most ordained ministers misstate or distort the truth about Jesus? If so, why do you think they do that?
3. Would focusing on Jesus being an "elder brother" to Christians and a fellow child of God help in witnessing to many nonbelievers?
4. How difficult do you think it would be to unify the monotheistic religions, including the various denominations of Christianity, with regard to the humanity of Jesus? What ideas do you have to help achieve this?

Chapter 9:
The United States as a Christian Nation—Not Really

History

Many claim the United States began as a Christian nation. It is true that numerous founding fathers professed to be Christians and/or were involved in a Christian church in some way. That does not make the nation a Christian nation, though. When the United States was formed, the country did not officially espouse Christianity, nor did it establish a state church as many other countries had.

Indeed, if one thinks of a Christian nation as being one that exemplifies Jesus' teachings on love even for one's enemies, treating all persons fairly, etc., it can certainly be demonstrated that this country's founding and history did not indicate Christian values. In fact, in some ways the Native American Indians were far more Christlike in the way they welcomed and helped the immigrants from Europe than the immigrants were in their treatment of the Indians.

Our nation was founded by stealing the land of the Native Americans, often killing them and sometimes enslaving them, in addition to damaging or destroying their property—as well as by fighting a war against the British for independence. Since its founding, the United States has fought in numerous other wars against various nations for causes that were sometimes questionable at best.

Furthermore, wars are only one of the indications of our country's lack of Christian principles. Slavery was widespread in the southern states during most of the first century of the country's existence. Women lacked the right to vote and were in some ways treated as second class citizens for the majority of our country's history.

In addition, our nation has often facilitated the marketing of harmful products by allowing false and misleading advertising worldwide. Alcoholic beverages, gambling, junk food, military weaponry, pornography, and tobacco are some of the things that are marketed and sold widely worldwide from United States points of origin via false and misleading advertising.

If the United States government eliminated the illegal and immoral activity by its own military, civil government, corporations, and individuals, I am confident that our nation would gain the support it needed from governments and individuals in other countries to win the war on terrorism. To many individuals in many countries, the United States is the terrorist.

Progressing Toward Christian Values

I do feel the United States is making significant progress in some ways toward practicing Christian values, despite apparently limited progress (or backsliding) in other ways. And, while I advocate freedom of religion for all, I do support the United States progressing closer toward exhibiting the genuine Christian values that many claim the country had at its founding.

Even many nonChristians would be happy if the country exhibited good "Christian" morals. Lots of Jews, Christians, Muslims, Hindus, Buddhists, agnostics, atheists, and many others agree on the need to be truthful, honest, fair, compassionate, etc.

How do we demonstrate these morals? For one thing, this country's government officials can do a much better job of empathizing with and sympathizing with other nations' residents in areas where we disagree. Let's devote more resources to international humanitarian aid, education, and negotiations—fewer toward military weaponry and wars. Is there any good reason the U.S. government should support (or bribe?) leaders of other countries to get oil (or other products) cheaply while allowing the rulers of those countries to abuse their residents?

Also, our government needs to do a much better job of stopping false and misleading advertising in this country—and by United States companies internationally. For example, if U.S. tobacco companies cannot advertise tobacco on certain forms of

United States media, ought they to be able to advertise in other countries using these forms of media?

Though I am a nonsmoker, I did smoke a few packs of cigarettes as a child, probably in the late 1960s. One likely reason is the persuasive tobacco advertising on television in those days—another, the easy access to cigarettes. Limiting tobacco advertising and limiting young persons' access to tobacco products could prevent many children from ever smoking or chewing tobacco.

I don't want to pick on tobacco too much though; both the use of tobacco and advertising for it are restricted significantly now (though more could be done). Also, tobacco is just one example of the numerous products our nation markets worldwide through unfair marketing techniques that do more harm than good.

Other countries are also guilty of creating or allowing false and misleading advertising (and other ethical violations), but is that any excuse for the United States to do it?

The United States and the world will both be better if the most influential country on Earth really does become a "Christian nation" in the good sense of the term. Let's seek to follow the golden rule of treating others as we desire to be treated. Yes, let's seek to "be good and do good," to offer an approximate English translation of words credited to Buddha many centuries ago. Being good and doing good seems to summarize Jesus' basic teachings and illustrate what being Christlike, a Christian, is all about.

We need neither have a state church nor even formally baptize citizens into a Christian church in order to establish a "Christian" nation that follows the marvelous teachings of Jesus and other great spiritual leaders. Following these quality teachings will, however, require commitment and discipline.

I think prayer and sincere faith in a higher power are keys, but I am confident there are many who lack faith in God who still seek to obey righteous authority, "God's law." Often these "nonbelievers" do so more successfully than typical professing Christians. And after all, isn't seeking and obeying righteous guidance what Christianity and other great religions are basically about?

Our country has progressed far during its over 200 years of history, passing laws to eliminate slavery, granting women more equal rights, establishing many humanitarian aid programs, and becoming more tolerant toward certain minority groups. Still, we remain far too materialistic, too self-centered, and too prone to fight wars against other nations. Indeed, our actions are often greedy and selfish.

In fact, many of us in the United States who claim to be Christians remain sinners who seek to keep on sinning. Perhaps even worse, we are in some ways self-righteous hypocrites who condemn the sins of other individuals (or of other nations) while ignoring our own (or those of our own nation). Although I don't desire to keep on sinning, doing wrong when I know better, I sometimes do. These sins include some times when I spoke or acted too self-righteously and/or hypocritically. I am trying to do better through the grace of God, and I hope others will, too.

You and I can do better than we have done thus far. Regardless of our formal religious faith (or lack thereof), I hope we all agree that there are some basic moral values that we need to learn and adhere to (compassion, honesty, respect for life, truthfulness, etc.).

Visitors to the United States from other countries probably often wonder why we behave the way we do. While I was a graduate student at the University of Kentucky over twenty years ago, one day I was talking with a wonderful international student who happened to be a Muslim. This individual asked me why so many Christians got drunk, smoked cigarettes, lied, stole, and engaged in fornication and why other Christians didn't seek to do more to correct those who did such things. I had no good answer. I don't remember exactly what I said in reply to the person, but the phrase in quotes at the end of this sentence is I think a reasonably accurate paraphrase of what I told the person: "I really don't know the answer, but many who claim to be Christians aren't really Christians, and even Christians aren't perfectly obedient to God, just trying to be, and it isn't easy to correct those who engage in such behaviors as those you mentioned." That individual's question was thought-provoking. I have thought about it often since. Indeed, I feel that if we "Christians" came much closer to practicing true Christianity, it would do much to ease the conflicts we have with Muslims.

I hope I don't sound too negative. From our nation's founding to today, the United States has been blessed to have many wonderful Christian people (and others) serving God for the good of the country and of humanity worldwide. The rebuilding efforts of the U.S. government and U.S. citizens around the world after World War II, even in countries that were former "enemies," are just one example. That rebuilding helped turn former enemies into allies, and it cost far less than it would have to fight a World War III. Currently, numerous international aid programs receive huge sums of money in donations from persons in the United States. Also, Christian missionaries, Peace Corps workers, and others from the United States help out worldwide. Our scientists, engineers, medical professionals, etc., have developed and used many modern devices that benefit citizens around the world.

Despite this, we still have far to go. May we please progress further along the path to righteous, "Christian" living?

If we don't progress in this way, our government may eventually be replaced by a socialist or communist government. In the next chapter, I very briefly discuss our economic and governmental systems and why greedy capitalism can lead the people to turn to another form of government.

Chapter 9 Questions for Reflection and Discussion
1. Why do you think so many "Christians" seek to perpetuate the myth that the United States practiced true Christianity as a nation in its early days?

2. Do you think stealing the land from the Native American Indians was justified as part of some predestined plan of God? If so, why? If you believe it was a sin, what do you think should be done to prevent something like it from happening in the future?
3. Are there parallels between the United States taking land from Indians and Israel taking land from other residents for its "Promised Land" as discussed in the Old Testament? If so, do you think one or both were right or were both wrong?
4. How could persons in past centuries who professed to be Christians justify slavery?
5. What do you propose the United States government do in regard to the marketing worldwide from the U.S. of things such as tobacco, alcoholic beverages, gambling, pornography, advanced military weaponry, etc.? Is it reasonable that U.S. companies and the U.S. military do things in other countries that are illegal here?
6. What can you personally do to help yourself and this nation progress closer toward righteous "true Christian living"?

Chapter 10:
Capitalism, Socialism, Communism, Geography, and God

I feel privileged to live in the United States, which is basically a representative democracy and a republic, under an economic system that is typically referred to as capitalism. In the sense that compassionate capitalism rewards those who work hard and honestly at useful work while ensuring care for those who are unable to do such productive work for various reasons, I think that our system is a far better system for practicing true Christianity than either socialism or communism. Majority rule with minority rights is nice, too.

However, I think it is wrong for true Christians to condemn socialism and communism as 100% evil tools of the devil. Indeed, I think that it is important to remember that the quality of one's life is determined to a large degree by factors other than the type of economic system and government rule that one lives under.

Living near the North Pole, in Antarctica, in a desert, or in numerous other locations that offer limited opportunities for growing and harvesting crops to eat and feature temperatures too cold or too hot for humans to live comfortably would likely be very tough regardless of the type of government. It might be a very difficult life.

In contrast, even a slave in a prosperous area might feel privileged. Indeed, in the Deep South of the United States just before the American Civil War some slaves perhaps lived under better conditions than the majority of the free people in the world. The best-cared-for slaves often had a house for shelter, plenty of food to eat, clothing to wear, etc. Due to the "Christian" beliefs of some of their masters, many even got a Sabbath Day of rest, as well as some leisure time on their six work days of the week. Sadly, some of those slaves may have been better off than some freed slaves at the end of the Civil War who lacked education, went north, and without education or job training ended up in city slums where some of their descendants may still live today.

Obviously slavery is wrong, and even if some slaves were treated relatively well (for slaves) in the early 1800s, they lacked their freedom and the opportunities that come from it. These slaves also lived a much harder life than the masters that owned them.

But a greedy form of capitalism that creates and enforces laws that keep most resources and capital in the hands of a few while the majority of working people struggle to earn enough to buy food or pay rent on an apartment is not necessarily always better. Far too many people are homeless and/or hungry here in the United States.

People may turn to socialism, communism, and other alternatives to capitalism when they experience the negative side of capitalism where resources are controlled by a small minority and the masses suffer in poverty. If private businesses seem to be abusing the masses, the people may seek a government that is less friendly toward private businesses.

In most of the United States, the vast majority of us are probably blessed with a nice climate, abundant natural resources, and many other blessings that we too often take for granted. Let's enjoy our blessings, but let's also seek to ensure that our laws and our economic system are fair to all. I think that is what God desires.

If we do right, our government and our country will prosper. And, just as a country in decline can revive, persons in decline can revive. Some even claim that human beings can rise from the dead, citing Jesus as an example. In the next chapter, I discuss resurrection from the dead.

Chapter 10 Questions for Reflection and Discussion
1. Do you think capitalism needs to be compassionate capitalism that cares for all people?

2. Do you think that if capitalism (or a democracy) fails to adequately meet the needs of every resident (or most people) that residents may replace it voluntarily with socialism, communism, or some other form of government that is less friendly toward private businesses?
3. What (if anything) do you think should be done to improve the capitalistic system in the United States?

Chapter 11:
Resurrection from the Dead Is Impossible—Or Is It?

For Jesus or anyone to rise to life again from the dead is scientifically impossible—or is it? There are a few well documented cases of persons that were thought to be dead who "came back to life" in their casket. Many more persons have "come back to life" in hospitals or houses in their beds. If you doubt my words, use Google or another Internet search engine to find some of the numerous articles online about these "miracles." Search using the words "dead come back to life;" omit the quotation marks to maximize the number of results.

Scientists may claim that these persons never really died and were mistakenly declared dead, but scientists can't prove that. Scientists and medical professionals don't know how the persons revived. We humans don't know what happened.

We do know that cardiopulmonary resuscitation (CPR) often can revive persons who have stopped breathing and whose hearts have stopped beating. In a sense, these are certainly cases of raising people from the dead.

Bible Stories

For nonbelievers, the Bible is not a valid source. But for Christians who believe the Bible, Jesus' resurrection is not unique. Other Bible stories about resurrections from the dead discussed in the King James Version include:

(1) Jesus raising a widow's son from the dead, as recorded in the New Testament book of Luke (chapter 7).

(2) Jesus raising Lazarus from the dead, mentioned in John 11.

(3) Ezekiel following God's instructions to "prophesy" to raise dry bones back to life, as recorded in Ezekiel 37—a far greater miracle than raising Jesus back to life after three days.

(4) Many dead "saints" rising up after Jesus' death on the cross, according to Matthew 27:52.

(5) Jesus' disciples raising the dead. Acts 9 states Peter revived Tabitha (also called Dorcas) from the dead. Acts 20 states Paul raised Eutychus from the dead.

Cloning a Mammoth? And "Dead" Seeds Germinating

In recent years, some scientists have been trying in a sense to raise a mammoth back to life by cloning one using DNA from cells that have been frozen for many years. Numerous news articles discuss this, including a 2011 article on Livescience.com (http://www.livescience.com/17386-woolly-mammoth-clone.html).[1] If it happens, this could be considered a "miracle," though I am not convinced such a scientific experiment is good for either us or the mammoth.

Perhaps an even greater miracle of raising the dead is the growing of a huge tree from a dry, apparently dead seed that has been dormant for a few years—or much longer. Some seeds even centuries old can germinate and become full-size plants when placed in soil, watered, and exposed to sunlight. I've personally planted a few seeds that were over a year old which grew into full size plants. Of course, from a scientific viewpoint, I guess even a century-old seed that germinates isn't considered "dead," just dormant. Could humans somehow remain "dormant" for three days or an even longer period of time? I don't know. I doubt that scientists know either.

Concluding Thoughts on Resurrection

I don't know whether Jesus actually arose from the grave as described in the four gospels of the New Testament. My personal Christian faith does not depend on whether Jesus came back from the dead, revived from a coma, or something else happened. I do feel, though, that the things discussed in this chapter indicate that resurrection from the dead may be possible in one sense or another. Unless proven otherwise, I think true Christians can consider Jesus' literal resurrection from the dead as at least a possibility.

If resurrection from the dead may be possible, what about a virgin birth? I discuss virgin birth in the next chapter.

Chapter 11 Questions for Reflection and Discussion

1. How do you feel about resurrection from the dead?
2. Does the Christian faith require believers to think that Jesus literally rose from the dead? Why or why not?
3. Is the parallel between a dry seed many years old germinating and a person being raised from the dead a valid one? Why or why not?
4. How do you feel about cloning? Is it ethically wrong? If so, what should be done to stop it?
5. Do you think medical science will someday develop a way to raise people from the dead (who have been deceased for a few days) and enable them to live relatively healthy lives for quite a while afterward? If so, do you have ideas on what ethical constraints would need to be put in place to prevent abuse, suffering, etc.?

Chapter 12:
Virgin Birth

Was Jesus born of a virgin? That is something many nonChristians consider impossible, but many Christians consider a basic foundational belief of their religion.

Personally, I believe that being a true Christian doesn't require one to believe that Jesus was born of a virgin, but I also believe that true Christians don't need to reject that belief either.

First of all, obviously Christians don't believe that Jesus was created instantly by God out of the dust of the Earth. The Bible states clearly that Jesus was born of Mary. Mary apparently carried Jesus in her womb in a normal way until the time his birth was due, as I interpret the Bible.

The Bible also makes it clear that Joseph (who became Mary's husband) was not the father of Jesus. However, this leaves open many possibilities.

One possibility is that somehow God was literally the Father of Jesus. But it is also possible that Mary was impregnated by someone else besides Joseph. Several Bible scholars who know much more about Greek than I do (Since I know no Greek, that doesn't take much.) note that the word translated "virgin" in most English Bibles in Matthew 1:23 and Luke 1:27 can also sometimes mean "young lady" or "unmarried daughter."

Furthermore, the passage in Matthew 1:18 (KJV) referring to Mary being ". . . with child of the Holy Ghost" doesn't necessarily mean God was the child's father. The word "Holy" used there (as well as in Matthew 1:20 and Luke 1:35) could mean that Mary did nothing wrong (was sacred or holy or pure) and that the child was due to rape, thus from Mary's point of view the child was a child of God rather than a child resulting from an act of fornication or adultery by Mary, as she was overpowered.

Also, according to many, the Jewish Talmud refers to Jesus as being the illegitimate son of a Roman soldier named Panthera. I know of no way to prove or disprove that scientifically. Indeed, we honestly have no way of scientifically proving who Jesus' father was.

At any rate, given the Old Testament Jewish laws against adultery and the severe punishment advocated for violating those laws, Mary and Joseph certainly seem to deserve to be commended for their commitment to the child and to each other.

Finally, scientists know today that "virgins" can become pregnant—through artificial insemination. Virgins who suffer from rape could also still be considered virgins in a sense, as could those who become pregnant through foreplay that results in sperm contacting one's hand, etc., then being transferred to the womb accidentally.

There is more than one way for sperm to intentionally or accidentally end up where it can impregnate a woman. I believe a virgin can become pregnant without God being the Father, and maybe (just maybe) that is what happened to Mary.

But under the Old Testament law, Mary possibly took a big risk by carrying Jesus in pregnancy before becoming intimate in marriage with Joseph. If found guilty of adultery, she could have suffered capital punishment. In the next chapter, I discuss capital punishment—and why I as a Christian oppose it.

Chapter 12 Questions for Reflection and Discussion
1. Do you believe that Jesus was born of a virgin? Why or why not?
2. Do you think it is important for Christians to believe that Jesus was born of a virgin?
3. What is your opinion about the view of some that a Roman soldier was Jesus' father?

Chapter 13:
Capital Punishment and Christianity

Over 2,000 years ago, Jesus died as a result of capital punishment, crucified under the orders of the Roman government. The fact that the founder of Christianity suffered through capital punishment is one reason I think Christians ought to oppose it.

Even Pontius Pilate (the Roman ruler who sentenced Jesus) apparently felt that Jesus had not committed a crime worthy of capital punishment. According to the New Testament gospels, Pilate submitted to the wishes of an angry mob.

Based on my reading of the New Testament, Jesus emphasized compassion and love—not hatred, revenge, or capital punishment. Remember that Jesus instructed his followers to "love your enemies" (Matthew 5:44, Luke 6:27; KJV). If I love my enemies, will I kill them? I don't think so. At least I hope I won't!

I urge Christians who support capital punishment to also remember the Apostle Paul. This highly respected leader in the early Christian Church wrote much of what became the New Testament. Before his conversion to Christianity, however, he supported the stoning of Stephen to death (see Acts 8:1). In addition, he persecuted other Christians, seeking their imprisonment and death (see Acts 22:4). Many likely felt Paul deserved capital punishment. But if Paul had been crucified then for his crimes, what would have happened? We would have missed out on his marvelous conversion to Christianity and his magnificent ministry. Let's seek to reform criminals, not execute them.

Capital punishment is especially tragic when persons receive the death penalty for crimes they did not commit. We have no human way of counting the number of innocent people executed over the years because of the imperfections of our justice system. Even today, who knows how many innocent persons remain on death row unjustly?

Too often, persons are sentenced to capital punishment as a result of emotional outcry that comes over widely publicized cases. Pacifying public opinion is considered more important than considering the rights of the criminal. When a particularly heinous crime is widely reported on television, radio, the Internet, and in the print media, calls for the death penalty for the criminal(s) responsible are widespread. Often many will call for the suspect(s) to be executed before even receiving a trial. That is not justice; it is much like the angry mob that called for the execution of Jesus.

Juries can be biased, too. In the United States, my understanding is that persons who oppose capital punishment are excluded from serving on juries in trials where the defendant is eligible to receive the death penalty if convicted. The reason of course is that those of us with such beliefs would never sentence someone to the death penalty. In my opinion, this may bias the jury before a trial starts by excluding many of the most compassionate people.

What About DNA Testing and Other Safeguards in the Justice System?

DNA testing results in freedom for some on death row, as well as for some persons falsely imprisoned for noncapital offenses. The Innocence Project's website (https://www.innocenceproject.org)[2] provides more information about this.

However, many others who may be innocent remain on death row. For those who think DNA testing prevents innocent people from being executed, I urge you to remember that even if DNA tests can be done and are done in a particular case, the DNA testing can be faulty. After all, fallible humans designed the test and conduct it. Even if the individuals conducting DNA tests do not deliberately falsify results, there are lots of opportunities for errors in the testing procedure—if not done properly. If you doubt this, use a search engine to do an online search for DNA testing errors.

Indeed, there are many problems with capital punishment and how the justice system currently applies it in the United States. Two of the numerous websites with more information about this are the websites of Amnesty International USA (https://www.amnestyusa.org/issues/death-penalty/death-penalty-facts/death-penalty-and-innocence/)[3] and of The Death Penalty Information Center (http://www.deathpenaltyinfo.org/documents/FactSheet.pdf).[4] These websites provide several reasons to oppose capital punishment.

My View and Recommendation

I respectfully disagree with those who claim that the death penalty deters crime. Did executing Saddam Hussein on December 30, 2006 for his past crimes help the situation in Iraq? I think not. In some cases, executing a criminal leads to increased crime (and more deaths) as the executed person's relatives, friends, and others respond by committing violence.

Even terrorists apparently frequently rationalize that they are administering capital punishment on persons for the past crimes of individuals, governments, cultures, etc. Violence that makes matters worse needs to cease.

Emotions must not overrule logic. I don't want lynch mobs rounding people up and hanging them without a fair trial. I also don't want criminals treated inhumanely after they are convicted in a fair trial. If we Christians believe that we are only sinners saved by God's grace, what right do we have to condemn others? Criminals can be placed in prisons to protect society from them and to rehabilitate them. Everyone deserves a chance to repent up until the point when God ends their life.

Emotional outrage is even worse when it leads one group of people to condemn another group of people that is innocent to death. Instead of one person suffering capital punishment, many may die. For example, following the September 11, 2001 terrorist attacks on the New York World Trade Center and the Pentagon, I read about and heard about many here in the U.S. condemning all Muslims and urging their deportation or execution. It is terrible that many persons judged a whole religious group based on the actions of a few suicide bombers. Since I am blessed to know some fine persons who are Muslims, I found this to be horrible.

Summary

As a Christian, I advocate the elimination of capital punishment for our fellow humans convicted of crimes. Our justice system needs to rehabilitate criminals—or at least imprison them under humane circumstances. Since it is only through the grace of God that anyone is saved, how can we condemn anyone? I submit that we should not, and that we leave capital punishment up to God.

In addition to controversy existing over administering capital punishment for committing crimes, controversy also exists over euthanasia. In the next chapter I discuss euthanasia and some other end-of-life issues.

Chapter 13 Questions for Reflection and Discussion

1. Can any Christian support capital punishment for criminals when Jesus commands us in the New Testament to love our enemies? Why or why not?
2. Is there any situation where a criminal would be better off dead than confined in prison and hopefully getting some rehabilitation, while society is protected from him or her?
3. If you favor capital punishment, what do you support doing to administer it more fairly and to prevent the innocent from being executed?
4. If you favor capital punishment, would you have advocated executing Saul for the horrible crimes he committed before becoming the Apostle Paul?

Chapter 14:
Euthanasia and End-of-Life Issues

Euthanasia is a controversial subject. I think it is one that true Christians can respectfully disagree with one another about.

Personally, I hate for anyone to suffer. If persons are terminally ill and/or suffering pain, etc., that cannot be relieved by human medical treatment, I would prefer that they be allowed to pass on to heaven rather than suffer, if they so desire, instead of being forced to wait on a possible "miracle" through divine intervention. However, it is often difficult for even medical professionals to truly determine when someone is terminally ill. Mistakes can be made. Also, it may be difficult to know if persons who are unconscious or in a coma are suffering pain. Furthermore, persons who are limited in their ability to communicate (due to inability to speak, poor hearing, limited eyesight, being in a coma, being under the effect of mind-altering drugs, etc.) may not be able to communicate their end-of-life desires or even indicate whether or not they are in pain in a way that medical professionals can comprehend.

Making life and death decisions isn't easy. I sympathize with medical professionals who must make such decisions regularly regarding their patients.

I think it would be a tragedy for a person who can't see, hear, or communicate effectively to live on against their will. If that person suffers pain, it would be even worse.

Therefore, I would advocate allowing euthanasia for myself or another person in such a situation. However, legalized euthanasia could easily be abused. For example, persons could be told incorrectly that they are terminally ill, leading them to wrongly decide on euthanasia. Furthermore, perhaps persons suffering from chronic pain would choose euthanasia when actually they could get relief with a pain-relieving drug or some other technique.

Unfortunately, persons often feel forced to make life and death decisions based on limited information. For better or worse, medical professionals, relatives, and friends often must make choices about ending lives, choices that aren't easy.

I would love for everyone to either be a happy, healthy, productive person forever or to pass on peacefully to heaven at the perfect time from natural causes without any suffering. But I think euthanasia serves a useful purpose in some cases. And, if/when euthanasia becomes officially legalized widely, it needs to be limited to cases where it is beneficial. That's my current opinion on euthanasia, and while I think my view is that of a true Christian, I think there is room for debate and discussion on this issue.

End-of-Life Issues

Regarding euthanasia and other end-of-life issues, I think it is good for persons to make their desires known in writing to friends, relatives, medical professionals etc., in advance. However, persons' views may change over time, and may even change at the time they face a life and death situation. If these views change at a time when the patient is no longer able to communicate effectively, perhaps nothing can be done in all likelihood to institute the change(s). Despite this risk, I think it is better to communicate one's desires in advance.

In addition to communicating one's desires about end-of-life issues, it is good to have necessary records available where they can be found (medical records, will, financial records, usernames and passwords to online accounts, etc.). Numerous sources provide details about what types of records need to be available and offer suggestions on where to keep them, as well as whom to entrust them to.

Also, plan ahead for things like whom you desire to receive custody of your children (if you have children) if you should pass on unexpectedly, your desired plans for funeral arrangements and burial, etc. You can specify much in your will about how to handle your estate.

Last but not least, while it is important to plan for and to prepare for end-of-life issues, our focus needs to be on doing God's work for our entire lives, as long as our lives may be. Even many terminally ill persons enjoy life, appreciate God's blessings, and serve God effectively. Let's enjoy God's blessings!

And only God truly always knows when one is terminally ill. However, sometimes I think God makes the fact of a patient's illness being a terminal one clear to the patient, one or more medical professionals, and/or one or more others. At other times, "miraculous" healings do occur, and they are one of the subjects discussed in the next chapter.

Chapter 14: Questions for Reflection and Discussion
1. How do you feel about euthanasia?
2. Do you think legalizing euthanasia would lead to a lot of abuse and unnecessary early deaths?
3. Do you feel that medical professionals, relatives, and friends must make life and death decisions regarding euthanasia now? If so, do you think they have adequate guidelines for doing so? If not, do you have specific suggestions on what to change about the current system?
4. Do you agree with the author that even true Christians may respectfully have different views on this issue?
5. Do you have a will? Have you made your views about euthanasia, your funeral, burial, etc., known to one or more others in writing? Are the records others would need to effectively handle your medical, financial, and other end-of-life issues readily accessible to those who will need them when the time comes for you to pass on?

Chapter 15:
"Miraculous" Healings and "Speaking in Tongues"

"Miraculous" Healings

Do "miraculous" healings occur? If you define "miraculous" healings as those that occur without any known human reason, yes, of course they occur.

You can read online about numerous cases where patients recovered when medical professionals had given up all hope of recovery for them. You may even know personally about one or more such cases.

If medical science advances further, maybe someday we will know scientific explanations for many of the "miraculous" healings. However, I believe that a higher power that I call God leads to many of these healings through prayer, etc.

I believe that it is difficult to investigate and verify the authenticity of many of the "miraculous" healings that allegedly occur in churches through the laying on of hands, anointing with oil, being "slain in the spirit," etc. But I am confident that some occur somehow in some way. Since many apparently devout members of churches where such things are practiced still suffer from chronic illnesses of various types, obviously such healings don't always occur for whatever reason, but that doesn't make those that do occur invalid.

On the occasions that I have visited churches where such "miraculous" healings allegedly occurred, I did not witness any healings that I felt sure were due to such a miracle. However, on at least one occasion when I was not in a church I personally experienced what could be considered a "miraculous" healing, which I discuss briefly below.

Personal Experience With a "Miraculous" Healing

One day when I was at work at a particular job, a worker who normally dressed nicely in business apparel was wearing very short pants. I looked at her with disapproval of her apparel and probably a bit of lust.

She looked back at me from where she was standing, perhaps 15 feet away, and said something like "I don't like the way James is looking at me. That's not like him. If he does it again, I'm going to hit him." I did it again, and then I felt a terrible eye pain, perhaps the worst I'd ever felt in my life. I prayed for relief if it was God's will. I prayed hard.

Soon afterward, another of my coworkers ran up in front of me; she was a Pentecostal Christian. The pain instantly ended. She said something like "There, is that better." I said something like "yes, thank you, God." I am confident that God somehow relayed my silent prayers to that Pentecostal coworker who served as God's instrument to heal me.

Later, the first coworker that I mentioned said to someone else that she was glad that second coworker helped me, that she would have removed that "curse" from me herself if she knew how since I appeared to be in such pain, but she didn't know how to do so. Apparently, one coworker put a "curse" on me, and another "healed" me. I considered it a "miraculous" healing.

Is "Snake Handling" Related to "Miraculous" Healings?

Some churches practice the handling of poisonous snakes, citing part of Mark 16:18 that states persons who "take up serpents" (KJV) will be protected by God. I am confident that God can protect us, as he protected the Apostle Paul when he happened to encounter a poisonous viper when picking up firewood on an island, as reported in Acts 28:3–5. But I feel that we shouldn't tempt fate by deliberately handling poisonous snakes. Furthermore, snake handling seems to be a bit cruel to the snakes—though I am much more concerned about the risk to human beings.

I know some snake handlers have died from their bites, based on media reports, but as to whether or not any have experienced "miraculous" healings after being bitten, I don't know.

Final Thoughts on "Miraculous" Healings

That one personal experience I mentioned earlier is enough to convince me that "miraculous" healings occur. But even without that incident, I have read about, heard about, and witnessed enough things to make it clear to me that numerous persons are healed in ways that medical professionals can't explain.

I also believe that many of these healings are from health problems that could have been avoided if we engaged in better health care practices. For example, I could have looked at that first coworker in a different way and have avoided the "curse" I received.

Let's all seek to be receptive to God for "miraculous" healings, but let's also seek to be obedient to God by practicing good health practices. God provides medical professionals and others (like that Pentecostal Christian who helped me) that can help us, but if we avoid problems by righteously obeying God it's even better.

"Speaking in Tongues"

In some churches "speaking in tongues" (sometimes called glossolalia or xenoglossia or xenoglossy or xenolalia) is common. I do believe that such a thing exists. But, personally, I believe that in most cases it is unnecessary, and without someone to translate what is said that it is not useful. And it is difficult to separate genuine cases from fakes.

I have visited some churches that practice "speaking in tongues." I'm not saying it isn't beneficial, but I did not witness any persons "speaking in tongues" in a way that I felt benefited the congregation or themselves. I have never spoken in tongues in a church, but on two occasions outside a church I did what could be considered "speaking in tongues." Below I discuss these two incidents.

One of Two Personal Experiences "Speaking in Tongues"

One of the two times I "spoke in tongues" occurred when I was a patient in a psychiatric hospital (I discuss my period of mental illness briefly in chapter 46 which is titled "Mental Illness (Bipolar Disorder, etc.)"). One of the staff members was questioning someone who was lying, and I interrupted the person who was lying to correct them.

The staff member looked at me and somehow did something that turned my words into gibberish. It was like she had figuratively twisted my tongue so that it wasn't moving the way I intended. I think the staff person then told me something like "Now, be quiet, I'm talking to them right now." I don't know what the staff person did or how she did it, but somehow she altered my voice without touching me.

Second of Two Personal Experiences "Speaking in Tongues"

The other incident when I "spoke in tongues" occurred when I was in the yard of a house. I was speaking to two other people. My thoughts were coming to me very quickly, and I was afraid I would forget my insights before I could express them, so I tried speaking faster and faster so I could convey them before I forgot them. Then somehow some "superhuman" power (God?) enabled me to speak very fast, so fast that my words sounded like gibberish, even though they were in English. I don't know how I managed to speak so fast that time.

Final Thoughts on "Speaking in Tongues"

I do believe that "speaking in tongues" exists, and I think that there are certain situations where it is a useful gift of God. However, in the two personal examples I cited above, I feel that other forms of communication would have been more effective. Similarly, I feel that most cases of "speaking in tongues" in churches are unnecessary. However, if persons who speak different languages can communicate with each other through the gift of being able to "miraculously" speak in one or more other tongues/languages, that is a fabulous gift of God. Such a gift may exist today, but I have not experienced it personally.

Regardless of whether or not you believe personally in such things as "miraculous healings" or "speaking in tongues," you are a beneficiary of another "miracle"—the miracle of your life's creation. It seems "miraculous" to me how human beings are formed and brought to life. And in the next chapter, I discuss being pro-life.

Chapter 15 Questions for Reflection and Discussion
1. Do you believe in "miraculous" healings? If so, do you think they come from God or from some other source? If you don't believe in them, why not?
2. Do you believe in "curses" and "cures" from them? If not, do you believe the personal experience the author described really occurred and how would you explain it?
3. What do you think about "snake handling" and the possibility of "miraculous" protection for those that handle poisonous snakes?
4. Do you believe in "speaking in tongues"? If so, what do you think causes it? If not, how would you explain cases like the two personal experiences the author describes in this chapter?
5. Do you think "speaking in tongues" involves/involved speaking in unknown languages, speaking gibberish, speaking one's native language very fast, speaking somehow in a foreign language for others to understand, more than one of the above, or none of the above? Please explain why you feel as you do.

Chapter 16:
Being Pro-Life, the Abortion Issue

Many persons advocate for the right to choose to have an abortion. I sympathize with those facing unplanned and undesired pregnancies. Often there is no easy solution to the problems that come from such pregnancies.

My guess is that in the early 1960s (when birth control pills became widely available) many stated that the pill would virtually end unwanted pregnancies. Unfortunately, many women using them did not take them consistently or properly. Perhaps even worse, when taken consistently and properly, birth control pills still were not 100% effective in preventing pregnancies. Furthermore, the pills had dangerous side effects for many women who took them. Despite improvements over the years, these pills still aren't 100% effective in preventing users from getting pregnant. Also, the "medication" still has harmful side effects for numerous persons taking it.

The easy availability of oral contraceptives likely encouraged casual sex and increased unwanted pregnancies. This probably increased calls for legalized abortion. At least that's my opinion.

Abortion is a symptom of the underlying problem of choosing to engage in casual sex. The unborn baby doesn't get a choice; it must trust its parents.

My guess is that many persons claimed that legalizing abortion for the early months of pregnancy would virtually eliminate the birth of unwanted children. These supporters of legalized abortion probably also claimed that it would greatly reduce child abuse.

For various reasons, however, many women who wanted no children did not get an abortion during the first few months of their pregnancy. Some then sought late term abortions. At least a few sought to kill their newborn babies. In addition, my guess is that child abuse is higher now than before legalized abortion came into existence, although reliable statistics on this crime are difficult to obtain. At any rate, legalized abortion has not solved problems as its advocates likely claimed it would.

What is next? Will parents who decide not to have an abortion but change their mind after the baby is born get a legal right to "abort" the child during the first week after the child's birth if the parents decide they don't want the child, can't afford to raise it, or don't feel qualified to care for it? Will persons claim that a child under a certain age (perhaps six years old or twelve years old?) cannot work enough to provide for its own food, shelter, and clothing—and parents have the right to "abort" them? Where does it end?

For many persons, I think the sanctity of human life is not what it used to be. It seems that people often desire to satisfy selfish sexual lust without following through with the expense and pain of childbirth or the time and trouble of raising a child.

Of course, for many women, when they feel that baby kicking inside their wombs, it is a special experience. They would find it hard to conceive of a circumstance in which they would murder that unborn baby. I think that is normal.

Persons who desire no children, I urge you to carefully read chapter 27, which deals with sexual abstinence until marriage. Even married couples who desire no children can demonstrate their love through methods other than sexual intercourse. Or, as an imperfect alternative, consistently and properly use multiple contraceptive methods (perhaps the birth control pill and condoms). Surgical procedures like a female sterilization or a male vasectomy are other options, though they aren't even 100% effective.

It might be virtually impossible to totally eliminate all legal and illegal abortions, but even proponents of legalized abortion would probably prefer to avoid the pain, expense, and health risks of an abortion whenever possible. I am confident that the number of abortions can be dramatically reduced through more persons practicing sexual abstinence, more persons using multiple forms of contraceptives, and more parents being willing to raise children or to give them up for adoption.

The sanctity of life is a very important issue as I see it. Do you agree with me that greatly reducing the number of abortions is a worthy goal to strive to attain as a part of practicing true Christianity?

One reason some oppose abortion is that they believe life is a gift of God, a creation of God. In the next chapter I discuss creationism.

Chapter 16 Questions for Reflection and Discussion
1. Do you agree that the invention and marketing of birth control pills likely led to an increase in the number of abortions and directly led to legalizing abortion nationwide, rather than reducing abortions? Why or why not?
2. Do you support the author's logic that legalized short-term abortions are leading many to also advocate for legal late-term abortions and maybe eventually many will also advocate for legal infanticide if the disregard for the sanctity of life continues its present course? Why or why not?
3. The chapter states, "even proponents of legalized abortion would probably prefer to avoid the pain, expense, and health risks of an abortion whenever possible." Do you agree? What (if anything) do you support doing to help reduce the number of abortions?

Chapter 17:
Creationism and Evolution Can Both Be Right Within Limits

The theory of evolution and belief in creationism can coexist within limits. Yes, I really believe that!

Evolution

Scientific inductive reasoning is a marvelous thing. But it has limitations. There is an old parable that apparently originated in India about six blind men who had never seen an elephant. Each of them touched a different part of an elephant and then described the animal differently based on the part they touched. They were unable to correctly infer what an elephant is like from feeling only one part, such as its side, tusk, trunk, leg, ear, or tail.

Scientists' assumptions about the past are based upon their observations during recent times. How can scientists claim to reliably describe events in the universe over a period of millions or billions of years, based only upon observations of life during a few thousand years on one planet in that vast universe? Indeed, what proof do we have that history even existed beyond those thousands of years?

Strong evidence exists for some aspects of evolution and the adaptation of species over time. That does not necessarily mean that human beings evolved from lower animals though. Human evolution remains only a theory—or maybe only a hypothesis.

An example of evolution's failings is the well-known story of Piltdown Man. In 1912, Piltdown Man was hailed by several scientists and many others as a major missing link that supported the theory of human evolution. To their credit, scientists began to question its authenticity. Decades later (in 1953) scientists acknowledged that Piltdown Man was a fake. Some of the world's best scientists were fooled for decades, though.

Of course, exposing Piltdown Man as a fraud did not disprove evolution. Scientists still believe that many archaeological discoveries both before and after Piltdown Man are genuine. What about the future, though? Since the Piltdown Man fraud managed to hoodwink scientists for decades, maybe scientists ought to be receptive to the thought that future advances in science may prove other archaeological discoveries to be fakes—or fossils misdated or misidentified through honest mistakes.

For example, assumptions of constant decay used in radioactive dating may be invalid. We have no way to know if such decay is constant over millions of years. We only have reasonably reliable written records of anything for a few thousand years. In fact, modern science has been around for only a few centuries—less than a century for truly modern science.

In addition, in recent years some scientists have expressed the belief that Homo sapiens had sex with Neanderthal man, as reported in numerous news articles, including a 2011 piece from Discovery News that is accessible on NBCNews.com (http://www.nbcnews.com/id/44277901/ns/technology_and_scienc e-science/t/how-sex-neanderthals-made-us-stronger/#.War6vch97IU).[5] If humans had sexual relations with Neanderthals, I doubt that humans evolved from them. Presumably, Homo sapiens and Neanderthal man both existed at the same time in order for that to happen.

Furthermore, even my old high school biology textbook (*Modern Biology* by James H. Otto and Albert Towle, 1973 edition; Holt, Rinehart and Winston, Inc., page 627) cited anthropologists as believing that Cro-Magnon man was a contemporary of Neanderthal man and perhaps "exterminated him" or maybe "Neanderthal man mixed with Cro-Magnon man and in time lost his identity." If Cro-Magnon man and Neanderthal man coexisted, obviously one did not descend from the other. Right? The theory of evolution is still evolving.

Over the years, scientists have made some big errors. In past centuries, they disbelieved persons reporting rocks falling to the ground from the sky. Scientists stated that there were no rocks in the sky. Of course, now scientists acknowledge their existence, calling them meteors (meteorites when they hit the ground).

Please don't misunderstand me. There is enough support for the theory (or at least the hypothesis) of evolution to come close to accepting some of it and to keep researching other aspects of it.

It's important, though, for science textbooks to mention that many aspects of evolution, including human evolution, are only a theory (or perhaps only a hypothesis), not fact. Scientists do not know how either the first life or the first human life originated.

Scientists need to be open to the possibility that human life (and life in general) came from some other method than evolution on Earth. Perhaps life originated on another planet and came here via a meteorite; maybe intelligent life forms elsewhere in the universe deliberately brought life to Earth. Indeed, maybe some life form elsewhere in the universe is so far advanced beyond us that in comparison to humans, God might be close to an accurate description of this immensely intelligent being from a human perspective. Or could it be that God created life on Earth?

Creationism

Belief in creationism (sometimes called scientific creationism or intelligent design) is held by millions, perhaps billions of people. Many are even willing to pay money to see exhibits related to it. In my home state of Kentucky, a Creation Museum opened in 2007, which has attracted a huge number of visitors.

Much about the way life develops and functions is unexplained, even by our best scientists. Indeed, life's original creation remains unexplainable. As far as we know, God or some higher power we can't identify or explain could be responsible for producing life.

While scientists cannot currently test creationism using scientific methods, a science textbook's chapter(s) on evolution can devote a paragraph or two to creationism's basic tenets and state that millions (billions?) of persons believe in it, while noting that current scientific methods can neither prove nor disprove it.

Personally, I'm a strong believer in freedom of speech within reasonable limits. I desire for the theory of evolution to be taught in our public schools. But I want it taught as a theory, not as a fact. And parts of the "theory" of evolution that are not very well supported by the available facts can be taught as a hypothesis, not even a theory. Creationism, however, also needs to be mentioned at least briefly, as do other hypotheses about creation. If textbooks only mention the theory of evolution, students may be much less likely to consider the possibility of alternative theories of creation. Isn't critical thinking about various possibilities something that the scientific method is supposed to encourage?

Someday creationists may be discredited like those who believed the Earth was flat. Instead, though, maybe evolutionists will be proven wrong, as they were with Piltdown Man.

For persons seeking to read about the numerous problems with the theory of evolution and about the alternative view of creationism, numerous resources exist online and in print. One detailed book you may desire to consider is *In the Beginning: Compelling Evidence for Creation and the Flood* (8th edition, 2008) by Walt Brown, who holds a Ph.D. in mechanical engineering from MIT. A shorter book to consider is *Creation: Our Worldview* by Grady S. McMurtry (5th edition, 2008). These two books (and others) make it clear that the theory of evolution has many problems. They also make a persuasive case for the Earth being much younger than most scientists believe it is.

Creationism and Evolution Are Not the Only Two Choices

Creationism and evolution are not the only two choices available either. As I stated earlier, perhaps some intelligent alien life form (maybe from beyond the Milky Way galaxy in the distant heavens) that is so superior to us that we might consider it God came and created this planet and humans, making Adam from the dust. So far though, we humans lack proof for any theory about the creation of life on Earth, whether it be evolution, creationism, or even little green men from Mars. From a scientific point of view, perhaps it might be better to call all these "theories" only "hypotheses."

Little Green Men from Mars Theory

In the late 1960s or early 1970s, when I was in elementary school, I considered the possibility that humans came from little green men from Mars. I heard or read references to little green men from Mars during my childhood, but never learned the origin of the references.

I read or skimmed most of the astronomy books in the Runyon Elementary School's library. If I remember correctly, I think all the books there that discussed the possibility of Mars having life as we know it or even water, either stated as a fact or indicated that the planet had neither life as we know it, nor water. Despite this, I thought that if scientists advanced further and studied Mars more or traveled there they might learn otherwise. I felt scientists knew little about Mars and might be drawing wrong conclusions based on very limited data.

Indeed, in recent years scientists have changed their minds. They now believe Mars currently has water and may even currently have some type of life. Scientists have learned enough since the 1960s to know they honestly don't know. Of course, I don't know either.

Final Thoughts

We honestly don't know how life originated on this planet—or elsewhere in the vast universe. Maybe both evolution and creationism are partially correct. Maybe something else is correct. My childhood hypothesis about little green men from Mars coming to Earth even remains a possibility (perhaps a very slim one, I admit).

Personally, I believe in creationism in the sense that I think some higher power (that I call God) created life as we know it. I also believe that at least to some extent evolution may have been the method used.

Yes, both creationism and evolution can coexist peacefully until we have more evidence. I think true Christians can accept both to some extent—at least for now.

Persons trained in scientific fields and persons whose studies focused on the Bible and its teachings may differ in their views on this issue. Each of us is unique compared to others.

In the next chapter, I discuss our uniqueness. The chapter focuses on how due to our individuality, even if we humans all benefited from the same opportunities, our individual achievements would be different.

Chapter 17 Questions for Reflection and Discussion
1. How hard do you think it is for the "theory" of evolution and belief in creationism to coexist?
2. Do you agree that the "theory" of human evolution is only a hypothesis? Why or why not?
3. How do you feel about the possibility that life on Earth may have originated on another planet?

Chapter 18:
Equality of Opportunity, Yes! Same Skills, No!

Great men like Thomas Jefferson and Benjamin Franklin read about different cultures and exposed themselves to a variety of ideas. Jesus and his parents (Mary and Joseph) probably gained much from their time in Egypt; Egypt apparently enjoyed much cultural diversity and wisdom at that time.

Perhaps the most talented persons are those who are multicultural. They benefit from learning in various environments and/or from possessing genetic material from various cultures.

Each individual is gifted differently. Each of us is better suited for certain tasks than for others. It's debatable how much these distinctions are due to heredity, environment, etc., but the distinctions remain a fact.

All persons deserve an equal opportunity to pursue success in any area. This equality of opportunity will not lead to total equality in all things, though. The elimination of discrimination will not lead to equal skills. Equality of opportunity to try out wouldn't mean a 59-year-old man who is about 6 feet tall (like me in 2017) would be picked to play center (or any other position on the court) for a team in the National Basketball Association. I'm glad playing in the NBA isn't among my goals.

If African-Americans make better athletes than Caucasians, they deserve more representation on professional sports teams, other things being equal. If immigrants from Vietnam to the United States score much higher on college entrance exams and perform much better in the high school classroom than Caucasians, Hispanics, or African-Americans, they deserve corresponding representation in the college classroom, other things being equal.

Furthermore, we must acknowledge that women and men often have different abilities. For example, only women can bear children or breastfeed them, and men are typically better suited for heavy lifting.

Also, we must be careful how we measure and judge human characteristics. For example, intelligence is not measured only in terms of formal education. My maternal grandmother only completed perhaps a couple of years of formal education, or maybe three or four. She probably could not read well. She did have many other skills, though. She could grow a garden, can her own food, use well water, and basically be more self-sufficient than most college graduates (including me). She also knew a lot of home remedies and the power of prayer.

Maybe our society will truly have taken a huge step toward eliminating discrimination when we no longer think of each other in terms of skin color, culture, race, age, gender, IQ test score, etc., but accept each other in terms of our overall individual characters and abilities, which depend on a huge variety of factors.

Discrimination takes many forms. Tragically, it is a major part of our history—and it remains today. In parts of the world, slavery even still exists!

I look forward to the end of all discrimination. In some future generation, we may almost all be multicultural like professional golfer Tiger Woods and President Barack Obama, as societal taboos against interracial/intercultural marriage vanish. Then maybe discrimination and affirmative action will both disappear. At that time, maybe we won't be arguing about equality, because we'll agree that we're all equal as human beings, but we are all gifted in different ways. Perhaps we will then be more accepting and respectful of those distinctions, too.

I have faith that it can happen. Interacting in a loving way with those of different races and cultures can help understanding. Maybe we'll even decide that the world will be better if a few persons decide to remain pure-bred members of their races (Caucasians, African-Americans, Native American Indians, etc.) due to the special gifts each race is given by God. But I think that is a decision to be left up to the personal choices of individuals—barring anything unforeseen.

Only God knows what the future holds. I am confident, though, that God desires the future to involve cooperation rather than violent conflict.

Treat everyone fairly, but preserve diversity. Fairness and equality of opportunity, yes! Equal gifts, no! It will be great when we can truly appreciate and enjoy the benefits of the diversity of the skills of various people. I think that is part of true Christianity.

Just as persons are not equally gifted, geographical locations are not the same. In the next chapter I discuss why providing city services to rural areas is not realistic

Chapter 18 Questions for Reflection and Discussion
1. How do maternity leave, breastfeeding, and the different strengths and weaknesses of men and women impact decisions on equal treatment? What changes do you advocate making to existing laws, if any?
2. Do you believe some cultures or races are genetically gifted to be better overall as athletes, scholars, etc., than others? If not, to what do you attribute current differences in abilities among them?
3. What limits (if any) would you place on equality?

Chapter 19:
Providing City Services to Rural Areas

Do practicing Christianity and observing the golden rule require providing city services even in isolated rural areas? I sometimes read about or hear about Christians (and others) seeking to provide city services to all (or most) rural areas.

It might be nice to enjoy benefits in rural areas such as city water and sewer service, city garbage collection, police departments, fire departments, hospitals, libraries, etc., when it is practical. Unfortunately, often it is not practical. If an individual lives miles away from their nearest neighbor, it would be enormously expensive to construct and maintain city water lines miles long for that one person—or one family. The same is true for many other services.

Often persons choose to live in an isolated rural area because land is cheap, they enjoy privacy, or they like living close to nature. It is wonderful that they can make that choice. They need to recognize, though, that making that choice necessitates limitations on the services that can be provided to them.

Even if it were economically feasible to provide city services to very isolated rural areas, the addition of these services might attract developments that would deprive the rural dwellers of the benefits they sought by locating there in the first place.

For persons living far away from others, getting water from a spring (or well) and disposing of waste via an outhouse (or septic tank) may be much more practical than paying enormous sums of money to install lengthy pipelines to pipe in potable water and pipe out waste.

Even today in the U.S., there are certain areas where telephone cables and electric power lines have not been installed. This is often due to the small number of people in the areas, the difficulty of the terrain, etc.

From a Christian perspective, I don't think it is appropriate or realistic to expect huge sums of money to be spent so that one family or a small group of people can enjoy the same services in an isolated rural area that city dwellers receive. Persons who desire city services can choose to live in a city or town. Persons desiring independence, a more natural environment, and a country lifestyle can choose to live in a rural area.

Each choice has benefits and drawbacks. I think both true Christianity and the golden rule advocate allowing persons to choose their setting and to accept its strengths and weaknesses.

Just as following God's guidance doesn't require us to provide rural areas with all city services, following God's guidance doesn't require us to always obey our parents. In the next chapter I discuss the Bible commandment to honor our father and our mother—and what it means.

Chapter 19 Questions for Reflection and Discussion
1. How can the needs of rural dwellers be met when offering city services to them isn't feasible?
2. If you support providing city services to more persons, what (if anything) do you advocate doing to make it more economical?

Chapter 20:
What Does It Mean to Honor Your Father and Your Mother?

It is fairly well accepted that one of the Ten Commandments in the Bible states "Honour thy father and thy mother. . ." (Exodus 20:12, KJV).

The meaning of the verse is commonly misunderstood to mean "obey your parents." This writer checked eight modern English translations. All used the word "honor" in that commandment in Exodus 20:12, except for the *Good News Bible* which used the word "respect." If you doubt me, check numerous translations yourself.

If translators intended to write "obey," I think they would have chosen that word. Obey and honor have different meanings.

We bring honor to our parents by doing the right thing, being obedient to righteous guidance. Blind obedience to parents who provide incorrect instructions can be dangerous (as can disobeying them in the wrong way).

The true story below from the author's childhood (perhaps described too fully) discusses a disagreement that arose from a Sunday School teacher's interpretation of this commandment and the author's reaction. (Note: Both the author's parents joined a church after he became an adult, and both demonstrated their love for the author in numerous ways during his childhood. Also, the Sunday School teacher mentioned in the next section was a good teacher, too.)

A Sunday School Teaching on Obeying One's Parents

One day a children's Sunday School teacher taught about one of the Ten Commandments, the one that states "Honour thy father and thy mother. . ."(Exodus 20:12 in the King James Version).

The teacher told the children that they should always obey their parents. One boy (me, this author) replied something to the effect "Which one should we obey? When your dad tells you to do one thing and your mom tells you to do another, it is impossible to do both."

The teacher said something like "obey one, then obey the other."

I responded by stating that sometimes both parents wanted me to do their particular thing right then. I was perhaps being a bit smart-alecky and stubborn in disagreeing with my teacher—but I prefer to use the terms precocious and steadfast to describe my behavior. After all, I sincerely wanted to know the commandment's meaning and how to obey it.

The teacher then asked me which of my parents brought me to Sunday School.

I replied that neither did, that I came with neighbors, that my mom and dad didn't attend church.

The teacher told me that she didn't believe me and that I shouldn't ever lie at all, but especially not in Sunday School class. She added that she was going to follow me to the church auditorium after class and talk to my mom and dad.

I told her she could follow me if she liked but my mom and dad were not there.

At the end of class, as I walked out of the classroom, I looked back to see if my teacher was following me. I didn't see her, but shortly after I entered the church auditorium and walked up to the couple who took me to and from Sunday School, my teacher walked up behind me.

The teacher asked the couple if they were my parents. When the lady replied they were not, the teacher asked if they knew my parents and could they point them out to her if they were there so she could talk to them.

The woman stated something like "His parents are not here. They don't come to church. He comes with us. But if he's doing something wrong, if you tell me I can tell them. His mom asked me to bring him to church because her husband doesn't like to come and she doesn't want to come without him."

The husband of the woman who brought me to Sunday School then spoke up. He said something like, "Don't go making the boy's dad look bad. Bill Gibson's a fine man. I work with him five or six days a week. Sunday is the only day he has to sleep late. I would not come myself if it weren't for you. Church is mostly for a women's social club and for children." His loud voice was probably heard by at least a few other people.

The Sunday School teacher said to the woman something like "no, I don't think he's doing anything wrong," and soon afterward excused herself, saying she needed to get back to her classroom to finish cleaning up. After taking a few steps toward her classroom, she stopped and turned around to look back. She seemed to convey inaudibly to me the spiritual thought that she couldn't do two things at once either, the thought that I probably would never again attend her Sunday School class, and that not coming back to it might be the best decision for me since many of her teachings would probably not be helpful for me.

I did not attend Sunday School again for a long time.

Reflection and Recommendation

After I became an adult, became a Christian, and was baptized, one day I reflected on the same commandment regarding one's parents that had troubled me that day as a boy, and prayed. I heard an inaudible voice I attributed to God telling me the commandment was not to obey my parents, but to honor them.

I opened a particular English translation of the Bible (and later some others) to check whether that was true. I found that in the King James Version, as well as the other English versions of the Bible I looked at, the commandment regarding one's parents did not use the word "obey." This made me (this author) feel better.

When one reads the Bible prayerfully and interprets it properly, I am confident one can gain guidance from God's Holy

Spirit. If I had been reading my Bible prayerfully as a boy, I likely could have gotten the answer I needed much sooner.

However, properly interpreting a Bible passage is sometimes difficult. Even an answer to a prayer needs to be tested to make sure the answer is coming from the Holy Spirit rather than a false spirit. The Holy Spirit will provide instructions to make a situation better; it will not tell you to do anything wrong.

Also, in this author's opinion, the New Testament is much more positively focused than the Old Testament. Some of the Old Testament teachings are difficult to understand—at least for me. If one has easy access to a knowledgeable human mentor and/or other written material besides the Bible that provide(s) very constructive guidance, that can help immensely in deciding what is the right thing to do in a particular situation.

In the majority of cases, children do right by obeying their parents. But for most (all?) children, there are at least a few occasions when parents disagree with one another—or agree but both give the wrong instructions. All families are dysfunctional to some extent. There are no perfect parents (or perfect children).

Boys and girls have an obligation to seek to obey God and not their parent(s) when they know God's directions differ from their parent(s)' instructions. Sometimes, however, it isn't easy for kids to realize that their parents are wrong. Even when children do realize that their parents are wrong, children may not know the best way to implement the right alternative—or even recognize what the right alternative is.

Therefore, parents ought to prayerfully seek to reach agreement on how to instruct their children. If moms and dads can't decide the right thing to instruct their children, how can the children be expected to have the wisdom to decide what is the right action to take? Divorces, remarriages, foster parents, adoptive parents, etc., can complicate matters even more.

Fortunately, help is available. Teachers, religious leaders, community leaders, neighbors, friends, and others can help provide basic guidelines and maybe even intervene on behalf of children and parents to help resolve problems. Perfect guidance for parents (and children) from other humans is not available, but very good guidance frequently is. I'm confident that when I was a boy there were several persons available in my town that could have provided quality advice to me (and my parents) to supplement the Sunday School teacher's instructions.

All God expects is for us to sincerely seek to do our best. If we prayerfully try to do our best, God through the Holy Spirit can provide perfect guidance—and the needed aid to follow that guidance. Seeking to do our best includes seeking to do good. Helping one another is more important than legalistically "obeying" a particular scripture. Far too many false teachings, incorrect interpretations, and harmful divisions exist within families and within churches. In fact, many nonChristians seem to follow the intent of the Ten Commandments better than many "Christians."

But if we all seek to listen, learn, help others, and to be ". . . speaking the truth in love. . ." as Ephesians 4:15 (King James Version) states, the world will be better off. Children honor their moms and dads by obeying them, unless there is a good reason not to. By obeying God, however, children always honor their parents. After all, when we feel that children are obeying God, the highest righteous authority, we credit the parents at least partially, for raising their children well.

As children and parents obey God, the highest righteous authority, God works things out for the best. Let's all seek to discern and follow God's perfect leading.

The Bible teaching to "honor" one's parents seems straightforward to me in its intent. Perhaps there is currently more controversy over the Bible's teachings about homosexuality. In the next chapter I discuss homosexuality, gay marriage and sexual lust.

Chapter 20 Questions for Reflection and Discussion
1. Read the commandment regarding parents in Exodus 20:12 in various versions of the Bible. Do you agree with the interpretation provided in this chapter?
2. What (if anything) do you think the Sunday School teacher could have done to handle the situation better?
3. What (if anything) do you think the author could have done to handle the discussion with the Sunday School teacher better?
4. How would you advocate teaching that commandment or answering a child's question about it?

Chapter 21:
Homosexual Rights, Gay Marriage, and Lust
(Heterosexual and Homosexual)

The hatred and bitterness that is often exhibited by some on sexual issues saddens me. We ought to at least agree to respectfully disagree.

It is important to distinguish between selfish sexual lust and love. Selfish sexual lust is wrong whether it is homosexual or heterosexual. Its purpose is to provide oneself pleasure without regard for the negative effects on others—or oneself. Love involves caring for one another.

As a Christian, I love all people including homosexuals. I consider homosexual lust wrong, but I also consider heterosexual lust wrong. The extent to which lust is wrong depends at least partially on the extent to which the lust is followed by a person's lustful physical activities with another person. As I see it, how well one controls one's sexual lust is more important than whether it is heterosexual lust or homosexual lust. Open public display of sexual affection seems to be disrespectful to others—and thus to God.

What Is Normal?

It is my opinion that heterosexual attraction is normal for most (if not all) people. During/after puberty boys and girls typically feel a natural attraction for the opposite sex. Eventually this typically leads to one male and one female becoming a couple. If this couple builds their relationship slowly, manages to avoid sex before marriage, and thus can develop their marital partnership for at least nine months before a child emerges from the woman's womb, I think it is wonderful. Chapter 27, "Sexual Abstinence Until Marriage Is Best," discusses this more fully.

A wedding traditionally formally unites a male and a female who are attracted to each other. Marriage (in theory at least) provides stability, love, and material support for the children of the married couple, in addition to a stable monogamous relationship between a male and a female. The normal way our species reproduces is for one man and one woman to join together in a way that produces a pregnancy and a child.

Do Homosexuals Deserve Marital or "Family" Benefits?

A primary reason that employers and the government provide family benefits to married couples is probably to ensure proper care for the children that result from a marriage, as well as for the spouse who is the primary caregiver for the children. Years ago, when birth control methods were less reliable and life expectancies were much shorter, it was common for women to be involved in child care for much of their married lives.

Two homosexuals cannot produce children from their own union, just between the two of them. As a result, I see no need for marital benefits for gay couples. Indeed, some family benefits for married heterosexual couples who both work and have no children are questionable, but in many cases at some future point these heterosexual couples will have children. Rather than specifically exclude benefits for the minority of heterosexual married couples who never have children by keeping records on a case-by-case basis, it seems reasonable to me to include family benefits for all married heterosexual couples.

Sexual Orientation Reversal?

Homosexuality is apparently far less common than heterosexuality and in at least a few cases has apparently been reversed. Various groups offer help for homosexuals seeking to voluntarily change their sexual orientation, but many questions remain unanswered about how effective this can be. Also, the scientific debate is ongoing over what causes homosexuality.

Personally, I am a heterosexual. However, I recall that on one occasion in a store, I saw an attractive female and looked the individual in the eye. Then I averted my glance and focused on a male and felt attracted to that person. It was as if I was for a moment seeing the male person through that female individual's eyes. This example indicates to me that individuals can transform from heterosexual to homosexual and vice versa.

Rights of Consenting Adults and the Government's Role in Marriage

I do respect the right of consenting adults to basically do as they desire in the privacy of their homes within reasonable limits—and this includes gays. But given the New Testament's opposition to homosexuality, I think it is wrong for Christian churches to sanction gay marriage.

I also oppose the government sanctioning gay marriage. Some claim the government has no role in defining marriage. I disagree. The United States Supreme Court set a precedent for defining a legal marriage more than a century ago by supporting laws against polygamy. In 1878 the United States Supreme Court decided in George Reynolds vs. the United States that Reynolds's religious beliefs as a member of the Church of Jesus Christ of Latter-day Saints (the Mormons) did not allow him to violate laws against polygamy. Laws against polygamy still stand, and the Church of Jesus Christ of Latter-day Saints has since officially renounced polygamy (supposedly partly due to a divine revelation in 1890).

Rulings in various courts (and new laws passed) in recent years have guaranteed homosexuals certain rights, including the right in the United States for homosexuals to get married. I think rulings that grant gays favoritism over persons who are single and celibate are incorrect.

I am a firm believer in the separation of church and state. Regardless of religious beliefs, though, I honestly feel that it is normal for human beings to mate as opposites, male and female. That written, I recognize that my personal beliefs as a single Christian may bias me. Though I wouldn't write it the way the Apostle Paul did in the New Testament, I basically agree with the Apostle Paul that homosexuality is wrong.

Concluding Thoughts on Lust and Sexual Orientation

This author believes that we are all loved equally by God, regardless of sexual orientation, just as God loves all creation. I personally have developed friendships with homosexuals—and I respect them. Many homosexuals claim to be Christians. Some even appear to follow Christ better overall than many heterosexuals.

If Jesus said anything about homosexuality, it is not recorded in the New Testament gospels. Of course, few words are even recorded from him there about heterosexual love. When he did speak about marriage, however, he seemed to assume it was a heterosexual male-female marriage, based on his words as recorded in the gospels. Also, Paul's New Testament writings and the Old Testament speak against homosexuality.

In summary, it is my belief that homosexuals deserve help, friendship, and love, but not marriage licenses. Allowing gay marriage might be a step toward legalizing polygamy, incest, and an "anything goes between two consenting adults" attitude that this writer feels would be far more destructive than constructive, in addition to discriminating against those who choose to remain single and celibate.

As I see it, allowing gay marriage or gay "family" benefits is a way of providing favorable treatment to one group that discriminates against those who are single and celibate or asexual. True Christianity involves treating people fairly, not offering one group benefits that favor them over others.

It would be great if the controversy over homosexual rights and all other controversies could be resolved fairly and peacefully. In the next chapter I discuss nonviolent conflict resolution.

Chapter 21 Questions for Reflection and Discussion
1. What is your position on homosexual rights?
2. How do you feel about gay marriage specifically?

3. Do you feel that heterosexual lust and homosexual lust are both wrong? If so, do you think both are equally wrong?
4. If you support gay marriage, how would you answer persons single and celibate who feel discriminated against by legalized gay marriage?

Chapter 22:
Nonviolent Conflict Resolution

If we humans would always resolve our internal, interpersonal, intercultural, and international conflicts fairly and peacefully, it might enable us to live happier, healthier, and longer. If the billions of dollars and the huge number of hours expended on wars and other violent conflicts were used constructively, this world could be a much better place. It seems terrible that so many persons are killed or injured due to violent conflicts. Billions of dollars of property damage occur, too. Wouldn't it be far better if conflicts were resolved without violence? If we were all true Christians, I think we could achieve such nonviolent resolutions to all conflicts—through God of course.

The solution seems simple. We could just seek to be fair to each other. But whole books have been written on nonviolent conflict resolution without solving the problem—and I certainly don't expect to resolve the issue in one short chapter. I do hope, however, that my words will be one piece that helps solve the puzzle of persons irrationally doing damage to themselves, others, and material possessions through violent actions.

One major cause of violent conflict is persons in positions of authority abusing their power. They commit violent acts and other abuses. Others often respond to this with violence. The cycle often repeats itself.

Obeying the simple but profound teachings of Jesus and Paul to love one's enemies could do much to reduce unnecessary conflict in the world. Trying to put oneself in another's shoes figuratively to understand things from their point of view might go a long way toward achieving this.

If someone becomes upset with me, I typically try (admittedly I don't always succeed) to figure out why they are upset with me. If I feel that their being upset with me is justified, I frequently will apologize and seek to take corrective action. Even if I feel that their being upset is not due to something improper on my part, my goal is to still try to listen to their point of view, try to understand why they may believe it is my fault that they are upset, and try to figure out a way to help them correct whatever the issue is. I seek to be helpful and to be humble.

If we let our emotions get out of control, it is very difficult to listen to and understand the other person, group, or nation. An important key to resolving conflict with others is keeping calm ourselves.

And yes, I think this principle can work on an international level. For example, instead of trying to intimidate another country into seeing things the way the U.S. government does and into doing what we here in the U.S. want, we could sincerely seek to learn and understand the other country's point of view and seek to obtain a just solution to the conflict.

Closing Thoughts

I may seek to write more on this topic in another book, if I feel God grants me specific insights that I consider appropriate. For now, I will simply conclude by stating that a key is a willingness by each person to seek to listen, learn, and apply what is learned to seek a fair solution, instead of seeking to use power to intimidate and dominate others, forcing them to do one's own selfish will.

Just as preventing conflicts from erupting into violence is preferable to having to end violent conflicts, preventing health problems is better than having to treat them. In the next chapter I discuss preventive health care. That chapter begins part III of the book, which focuses on specific behaviors of true Christians.

Chapter 22 Questions for Reflection and Discussion
1. What do you do to try to avoid violent conflict?
2. How realistic is it to use nonviolent conflict resolution methods for all conflicts?

3. What can be done to resolve minor differences fairly before they escalate into big problems and violence?

This chapter concludes Part II. Before moving on to Part III, please take time to review Part II. The questions below may help.
1. Do holding special attitudes and beliefs help separate a true Christian from an imposter? If so, how?
2. Are the attitudes and beliefs listed in these chapters appropriate for Christians?
3. What attitudes and beliefs (if any) would you add?
4. What (if any) attitudes and beliefs would you omit?

Part III: Specific Behaviors

Chapter 23:
Better Preventive Care—True Health Care Reform

I would love to see what I consider a "true Christian" approach to health care reform, or at least something close to it. While I commend the efforts by numerous people in government offices and other organizations to reform health care, I feel quality health care reform involves much more—and it often needs to occur at the individual level.

I am confident that true health care reform is attainable. We can enjoy better health and live happier, longer lives while spending less money on health care than we do now.

How? The key is to take better care of our health. Let's seek to prevent most health problems, so it won't be necessary to try to fix them.

In many (most?) cases, the best modern medical science can do (despite its marvelous advances) is to either treat symptoms or to provide medications and other treatments that help our bodies' own systems heal us. Let's seek to avoid getting sick so that we don't need professional medical treatment.

Often our own lifestyle choices lead to our health problems. By doing a better job of taking care of ourselves, we avoid many health issues.

People talk about the importance of health insurance. Indeed, health insurance can be extremely valuable. But the happiest and healthiest people are often those fortunate enough to avoid needing to seek professional medical care—regardless of the health insurance coverage they possess or their lack thereof. I am very grateful for my health.

Christians may desire to read and meditate prayerfully on I Corinthians 6:19-20, which discusses the human body. I am not a medical professional, so I can't give any medical advice. However, below I suggest some specific steps that I consider part of quality preventive care.

1. Tobacco

One step is for everyone who uses tobacco products to quit the tobacco habit. Tobacco use contributes to many illnesses and deaths. Fortunately, lots of programs exist to help tobacco users overcome their addiction. Please take advantage of one or more of them. I am hopeful that tobacco use can be virtually eliminated in one or two generations.

2. Alcohol

A second step is to avoid abusing alcohol. You are probably already aware that a huge number of traffic fatalities are due at least in part to alcohol intoxication and that alcohol contributes to many deaths resulting from various diseases.

If you already drink, please only drink in moderation, one drink daily or less for women and two daily drinks or less for men.

In Chapter 30 I provide more details on alcohol's harmful effects and explain why I feel even drinking socially in moderation has risks that outweigh any benefits.

3. Prescription Drugs and Illegal Drugs

A third step is to avoid abusing prescription drugs and illegal drugs. The number of deaths, injuries, and illnesses caused each year from abusing drugs is far too high. Please only use prescription drugs when necessary and in appropriate dosages. Avoid using illegal drugs, except in case of a medical emergency—if such a medical emergency is possible.

Whenever reasonable, seek to treat illnesses without taking any medication at all. Improving one's diet, getting proper exercise, getting adequate rest, and avoiding too much stress can be as effective as medicine in some cases. I discuss these things in later sections of this chapter, beginning with diet.

4. Diet

A fourth step is to eat a nutritious diet that includes a variety of fruits, vegetables, whole grains, beans, lentils, nuts, seeds, etc. Many illnesses can be prevented, cured, or have their severity reduced by a proper diet. For example, many diabetes cases can be treated effectively by altering one's diet, without taking medication. As I stated earlier, however, I am not a medical professional and cannot give medical advice. I am not a dietician either, so I cannot give professional dietary advice.

But the United States Department of Agriculture's website (http://www.usda.gov/wps/portal/usda/usdahome?navid=DIETARY_HEALTH&navtype=RT&parentnav=FOOD_NUTRITION)[6] provides numerous webpages with information on dietary health. For those on vegan or vegetarian diets, some helpful advice on dealing with "potential health problems" is provided on the MedicineNet.com website (http://www.medicinenet.com/vegetarian_and_vegan_diet/page2.htm).[7] Personally, I've been trying to adhere to a vegan diet for a few years. In chapter 31 I discuss some benefits of a vegan diet.

5. Exercise

A fifth step is to get adequate exercise. Just walking around one's neighborhood seems to be beneficial. I enjoy walking my neighborhood, taking nature hikes, and bicycling.

I don't think it is necessary to join a gym or do strenuous exercise. But again, I am not a medical professional and cannot give any medical advice.

6. Rest/Insomnia

A sixth step is to get adequate rest. Allow for eight or nine hours daily for sleep—or whatever is appropriate for your individual needs.

Two things that keep me awake at times are: (1) worrying about things I need to do the next day and (2) fears that I will oversleep. I help solve the first problem by making out a "To Do List" for the next day and placing it near my bed. If I think of something to add to the list after I get in bed, I add it to the list, then seek to forget about it and focus on positive thoughts in a prayerful spirit.

I help solve the second problem by setting three alarm clocks—the third one being a very loud one far enough away that I have to get out of bed to shut it off. I also try to get to sleep early enough to get adequate rest to wake up naturally before the first alarm clock goes off. Seldom do I need the second or third one, and I usually wake up before the first one goes off. But I set them to be safe, if I think I might oversleep for something important.

Maybe what works for me will help you, too. If not, investigate and see what works best for you.

7. Stress

A seventh step is to avoid excessive stress. Walking can help alleviate stress in many cases.

Nature hikes or quiet walks in a park help me relieve stress. They enable me to get away from the source of the stress and often provide me the peace of mind to rationally decide how to deal with the stressful situation when I return to it.

Getting in a quiet place and praying—often accompanied by prayerfully reading a spiritually uplifting book—often has benefitted me. Prayer and meditation can help.

In a lot of cases, situations that cause unnecessary stress can be avoided. I am blessed since I usually experience very little stress, overall.

Unfortunately, that's not true for many persons. In fact, often people seem to get a great deal of stress from dealing with other family members or their jobs. In such cases, communicating more openly (in a polite way) with others can often help to relieve stress and its underlying causes. Numerous resources are available that discuss stress and how to deal with it. I hope you find the right one(s) for you.

8. Risky Behavior

An eighth step is to avoid unnecessary risky behaviors. A few examples of risky behaviors are: skydiving, white water rafting, skiing, talking on a cell phone while driving, and operating dangerous machinery without proper training or safety equipment.

Fun doesn't have to involve big risks, but for many people their most dangerous times are their leisure hours. We all could do a better job of avoiding unnecessary risks.

9. Water

A ninth step is to drink adequate water to stay hydrated and flush impurities from one's system. Water is the number one component of the body. Water is the drink we need most. Water meets our needs much better than coffee or carbonated soft drinks.

Juices, sports drinks, and decaffeinated green tea in moderation are likely a nice supplement to water intake, though. Personally, I usually drink several glasses of water daily, a cup or two of juice, and in hot weather a sports drink. I plan to drink decaffeinated green tea more often, too, maybe a cup a few times a week, since numerous sources seem to advocate drinking green tea in moderation.

10. Education, Books, and Medicines

The tenth step is learning more about health care, acquiring one or more books on health care, and obtaining medications for use when needed.

To acquire a basic education on how to prevent (and treat) diseases and injuries, read online and at your local library about ailments that your particular lifestyle, work, genetics, etc., make you susceptible to. A wide variety of materials are available that you can probably browse at your local library or bookstore. You can also search online for numerous resources.

Buy at least one quality book on health care that contains tips on first aid and basic home treatment of diseases and injuries. If you think the Internet can replace the need for a book, think again. Even if the information is on the Internet and you know how to find it, the Internet is sometimes inaccessible, due to electricity outages or other problems.

Pick an up-to-date book that meets your personal or family needs, perhaps after getting recommendations from friends or medical professionals. I will repeat once again that I am not a medical professional and can't give medical advice. But I have found a small 1992 book of home remedies (*Physicians' Book of Home Remedies* by Bernie Ward; Globe Communications Corp.) very helpful over the years. I have also benefited from a 1993 *American Red Cross Standard First Aid* manual that has almost certainly been updated at least a few times since 1993. I also have a few more up-to-date medical resources, although I may need to take my own advice and buy a new medical book.

It is also a good idea to keep some basic first aid items on hand in your home. What to buy in advance depends on your particular needs and your budget. However, you probably want to have some adhesive bandages of various sizes, aspirin, a nonaspirin pain reliever, triple antibiotic ointment, hydrogen peroxide, alcohol, allergy medication, cough syrup, and a few other items. Note that all the items I listed above are relatively inexpensive compared to the cost of many prescription medicines.

What if you get ill and need medicines you don't have? Home remedies often work—remember the book on home remedies that I mentioned earlier? When home remedies don't work, a visit to a local pharmacy may lead you to over-the-counter medications that are suitable for what ails you—and a friendly pharmacist may even have time to offer some advice on over-the-counter medications if he or she isn't extremely busy. Please be respectful of the pharmacist's time, though. In addition, it may be necessary to phone a doctor or other medical professional to schedule an appointment, to visit a walk-in clinic, or even to visit a hospital emergency room.

But personally, I think we in the United States (and perhaps many other countries) often take too much medicine. Therefore, I emphasize better preventive care as the foundation of health care reform.

Conclusion

There are currently no manmade cures for many illnesses and injuries. Even the best medical professionals with the best equipment cannot restore one's health in some cases. Therefore, I hope and pray that we all seek to take better preventive care of our health. And, yes, I believe in prayer.

In fact, as a Christian I am a firm believer in prayer. I feel that many times prayer has resulted in "miraculous" healings for various people, when medical science failed them. But I also firmly believe that skilled medical professionals are a gift from God to help treat various ailments.

Furthermore, preventing those illnesses and injuries from occurring (or reoccurring) due to engaging in good preventive health practices is far better in my opinion. I recall reading that Jesus instructed a man he had healed to ". . . sin no more, lest a worse thing come unto thee." (John 5:14, KJV). That is good advice for us, too. Regardless of whether one is a Christian or a follower of another faith or of no faith, it is wise to avoid behaviors that do harm to one's health whenever reasonably possible.

Buddha is credited with stating words that translate into English as basically meaning "be good and do good." If we do this and try to follow the golden rule that is a foundation of Christianity and many other major religions, we can help ourselves and others to live healthier, happier lives.

Though preventive care in my opinion is the most important key to quality health, I also support a single-payer health care plan for basic health care coverage in the United States. I even support providing a reasonable amount of health care coverage for preventable illnesses and injuries under such a plan. Persons desiring additional health care coverage beyond the basic coverage in my proposed single-payer plan could buy it from a private insurance company. Persons capable of doing so could also pay via cash, check, debit card, credit card, or another method acceptable to a health care provider. Friends, relatives, religious organizations, charities, etc., could also help out in some cases.

Ideally, I would love for everyone to receive 100% of all their health care needs met regardless of the cost. But limitations on the availability of health care and the means to pay for it prevent this. However, if we engage in better preventive care to reduce unnecessary medical expenses, we can progress toward the point where medical resources are adequate to meet medical needs.

But for my health care vision or any health care reform plan to work well, it needs to be accompanied by human beings being committed to taking better care of ourselves, in my humble opinion. I hope we will commit to better preventive care—and succeed in attaining better preventive care!

One key to paying health care costs is to keep lots of people working productively to generate the revenue to pay health insurance costs and/or directly pay health care costs. In the next chapter I discuss a Christian work ethic, which I think is part of this.

Chapter 23 Questions for Reflection and Discussion
1. Which of the ten steps toward better preventive care listed in this chapter do you do well? Which do you need to improve substantially on?
2. Are there any of the ten steps you would modify or omit? If so, which one(s) and why?
3. What (if any) step(s) would you add to the list?
4. How do you feel about a single-payer health care plan for basic health care coverage?

Chapter 24:
A Christian Work Ethic, Unemployment Benefits, and Retirement

Whenever possible, I feel true Christians would prefer to be working at a job that helps others, instead of being idle. However, unemployment benefits can be a wonderful blessing. They help persons temporarily out of work meet basic living expenses.

Similarly, different programs benefit the elderly, disabled, caregivers of preschool children, and others who are unable for various reasons to work at an income-producing job.

But, unemployment benefits (and benefits from other programs) are not designed to let able-bodied persons sit idly at home drawing a government check instead of performing some useful service. Unemployed persons can devote time to seeking a job, doing volunteer work for a church or other organization, and taking constructive actions to develop skills in whatever way is reasonably available.

If you suffer from depression or some other problem, get help. Need job skills? Job training programs are available. Also, if your geographical area lacks job opportunities, please consider relocating.

I believe persons typically live happier, healthier, and longer if they are productive, doing something that benefits themselves and others. If you doubt my belief, check online and you can find numerous articles about scientific studies that indicate the same thing.

I encourage persons drawing unemployment benefits not to wait for their benefits to run out. Instead, search for jobs, do volunteer work, read informative books and other literature to better oneself, etc.

I've been blessed to always either have a job or to have friends and family who voluntarily helped me out, in addition to access to other resources that enabled me to get by without ever seeking or accepting unemployment benefits. I am grateful for that help and hope it freed up funds to help others who needed unemployment benefits more.

By the way, I don't want the unemployed to be forced to take any available job. For example, due to my personal beliefs, I would not want to work in a liquor store selling alcoholic beverages. As basically a pacifist, I wouldn't even desire to work in a military job, though I commend the numerous soldiers who serve faithfully: establishing peace, keeping the peace, doing good humanitarian work following natural disasters, etc.

Though I don't urge persons to take any available job, I do urge the unemployed to seek to find a job. Seek to "find a need and fill it," to quote words credited to Ruth Stafford Peale, wife of Norman Vincent Peale.

Folks, please use unemployment benefits wisely, and only when necessary. Private companies and the government do not have unlimited resources. The resources expended on unnecessary unemployment benefits could be used for something else, maybe even pay raises for workers.

By the way, one of the saddest things about unemployment benefits is that many of the people who in theory might need them most are ineligible due to not working enough hours per week at a job prior to becoming unemployed, not working long enough at a company, being self employed, etc. Furthermore, some employers seem to seek to avoid paying unemployment benefits by extensively relying on temporary employees, part-time employees, etc. Abuse of unemployment benefits is a problem among both employees and employers.

The system definitely isn't perfect. The people who have been actively but unsuccessfully seeking work, struggling to get unemployment benefits, and meeting numerous obstacles and major financial difficulties know that better than I do.

Despite this, I am very thankful that we have a system—and that it is probably much better than whatever system existed centuries ago. Please don't abuse it. If you are drawing unemployment benefits and are able to work, please actively seek work—and don't just "go through the motions." Perhaps try doing it like it's a full-time job that requires a lot of effort. After all, in a sense it is, as numerous writers of articles and books on searching for a job point out, and as many unemployed people find out.

Retirement

Even after retirement, the happiest and healthiest people seem to be those who remain active doing volunteer work or performing some other useful function. A Christian work ethic leads a person to be happily doing something beneficial until God calls him or her home.

I hope I will always be willing and able to do useful work as long as I live—and enjoy doing it. It is a blessing to be doing labor I enjoy that benefits others as well as myself. I am truly blessed to be doing a job I love (writing) and over the years have enjoyed a variety of nice second jobs to help keep the monetary bills paid. I hope you are all similarly blessed with productive, enjoyable jobs!

One thing that helps persons enjoy work more is having a career that they love. In the next chapter I discuss choosing a career.

Chapter 24 Questions for Reflection and Discussion
1. How widespread do you believe abuse of unemployment benefits by employees is?
2. How widespread do you believe abuse of unemployment benefits by employers is?
3. What are your plans regarding retirement?
4. Would you prefer remaining active at least part-time at a job you enjoy doing instead of retiring?

Chapter 25:
Choosing a Career

Christians who find the career where they can best serve God and others, thus making themselves happy in the process, are blessed. Choosing a career is an important decision and one that should not be rushed into. Furthermore, even after a career is chosen, one can alter that decision later and progress in a much different direction if so desired.

My Personal Experience

Perhaps the first time I seriously thought about careers was one day in the eighth grade. I don't remember the exact words of my English teacher. But I think the instructor basically stated that it would be good if we started thinking about careers. The teacher said we had plenty of time to think about it and certainly didn't need to make a decision that year. But we were provided a list of numerous careers we could look over. Then each of us could choose a few (five I think) that we were especially interested in and get a printout with more information about them. As I recall, my choices were freelance writer, lawyer, geologist, industrial engineer, and mining engineer.

Sometime after that, I think during my freshman year of high school, I read more about careers and learned that one of the best job opportunities was for individuals with a B.S. degree in engineering and an MBA. I chose that path.

However, in college I was not very good at Calculus or Physics, two key areas of study in engineering. I performed much better in the business classes for the MBA program, though I dislike what often seems like a dog-eat-dog business world, as well as many aspects of marketing.

I am glad I researched careers. But I regret paying so much attention to job opportunities and so little to passion.

Since childhood I have loved to read and write. But since the printout I received in school stated that job opportunities were sparse for freelance writers, competition was fierce, and pay was low (as I already suspected), I abandoned my first love.

I believe firmly that if I had majored in Journalism or Communications in college and devoted hours to developing my writing skills, I would have become a successful freelance writer many years ago, or at least become successful in a related field.

Still, I am pleased overall with my education. I learned a lot from a variety of classes. I also gained much from attending several seminars and lectures in college, as well as from participating in a wide variety of other activities that broadened my perspective.

I took several English courses as electives during my undergraduate studies. Then, while enrolled in Graduate School, I took some graduate level Communications courses. I also benefitted from taking a variety of electives in other areas during both my undergraduate and Graduate School years.

Recommendations

I urge persons seeking a career to consider their passions and interests, as well as the job opportunities for various career paths. Also, pay attention to your aptitudes and abilities. Passion and hard work can overcome much, but each of us enjoy (and lack) certain aptitudes and abilities. For example, a short person almost certainly couldn't successfully play center in the National Basketball Association; even very few tall individuals could.

I urge persons to seek a well-rounded education centered on obeying the highest righteous authority, God, thus doing the right thing. Though I considered college a priceless experience that I treasured highly, I realize that there are other forms of education that may appeal more to others.

For example, some people might benefit from going to a trade school, being an apprentice, or gaining on-the-job experience in some other way. For others with great discipline, it might be possible to acquire a quality education through reading extensively from resources available at libraries, observing others, and questioning professionals in various fields, etc.

My main point is that God desires each of us to develop our skills and to use them wisely. I think this requires thoughtful preparation and a willingness to adapt or even totally change directions as our knowledge and wisdom increase and/or circumstances change. Persons even in their 60s or 70s (or older) embark upon new careers.

I am happy with my current career as a bivocational freelance writer and with my plans for the future. However, I seek to be receptive to any changes God desires to make to my plans. I hope you, too, will be happy with your plans and be receptive to God's guidance for possible changes to them.

Regardless of your career choice, it is important to manage your earnings wisely. In the next chapter I discuss budgeting.

Chapter 25 Questions for Reflection and Discussion
1. How did you choose your career, if you have one? Are you happy with your career? If not, are you willing and able to make it better or to change careers? Why or why not?
2. What specific advice would you give to persons seeking to choose a career?

Chapter 26:
Budgeting

Being good stewards of the money we receive is part of practicing true Christianity. We don't want to worship money or to place too much importance on it, but it comes in handy for paying for our food, shelter, health care, etc.

I am a firm believer that God can take care of all our needs if we put God first (See Matthew 6:33, which is one of my favorite verses.). But I think following God's guidance leads to us acquiring money honestly and using it wisely. Finding the right career, which I discussed in the last chapter, helps lead us to acquiring money honestly.

Using money wisely means budgeting in one form or another. We typically must pay for our housing (rent, mortgage, utilities, etc.), food, clothing, and various other items.

Numerous books and other resources provide guidelines for making out a budget and sticking to it. I won't provide a lengthy detailed description of how to do it here. But I urge persons to seek to limit their spending to what is necessary, so that they have more available to use to help others, etc.

If you don't already, try making out a monthly budget, listing all your expenses and your income, then add in an appropriate amount to budget for expenses that occur less often than monthly (quarterly, semiannual, and annual expenses), and think about expenses that occur at unexpected times (replacing a kitchen appliance that breaks, repairing your car if you own one, health care needs, etc.).

If you know about how much money you typically make each month and about how much you typically need each month for housing, food, and other expenses, it can help you decide how to manage your money so that your cash spent doesn't exceed your cash coming in. It may even be advisable to downsize your housing, eat more beans and rice, etc. Also, please try to budget for donating to the needy and for unexpected expenses.

Remember that budgeting is only part of the process. Unexpected expenses related to health care, etc., can occur at any time. Also, unexpected loss of income due to a job layoff, etc., can occur. These changes may require modifying the budget substantially, seeking new sources of revenue, etc.

Ultimately, all we can do is seek to do our best and trust God for the rest. But I hope the information provided in this brief chapter helps you to be good stewards of the money you earn through the grace of God.

One big expense for many persons is the cost of bearing and raising children. Practicing sexual abstinence before marriage can delay parenthood and prevent sexual transmitted diseases as well. In the next chapter I discuss why sexual abstinence before marriage is best.

Chapter 26 Questions for Reflection and Discussion
1. Do you make out a budget regularly? If not, will you consider doing so now?
2. After a budget is made out, unexpected expenses and unexpected loss of income can occur. Would you be willing and able to easily make substantial cuts in expenses and/or seek new sources of revenue if unexpected expenses and/or loss of income occurred?

Chapter 27:
Sexual Abstinence Until Marriage Is Best

Though the Bible speaks against adultery and fornication, logical secular reasons exist also for limiting oneself to a monogamous sexual relationship within a marriage. Why should a person risk a lifetime of pain and suffering for the sake of a few minutes of sexual pleasure? A sexually-transmitted disease or a pregnancy can result from just one sexual encounter.

There is a major difference between sexual lust and love. True love (which involves genuine commitment) can wait, as it will last a lifetime.

What happens if a sexually active single becomes pregnant? It isn't easy being a single parent. Also, even those who are pro-choice would prefer avoiding the expense, pain, and health risks of an abortion. Furthermore, carrying a baby for nine months then giving it up for adoption can likely be an emotionally wrenching experience.

Sexually transmitted infections (STIs) are another major concern. The U.S. Department of Health and Human Services website, Womenshealth.gov (http://womenshealth.gov/publications/our-publications/fact-sheet/sexually-transmitted-infections.cfm),[8] contains much information on STIs. Among many other things, the website states in an article last updated in 2009 that "In the United States about 19 million new infections are thought to occur each year." It notes that "almost half of new infections are among young people ages 15 to 24." The site adds that "STIs are spread during vaginal, anal, or oral sex or during genital touching. So it's possible to get some STIs without having intercourse. Not all STIs are spread the same way." Womenshealth.gov also points out that "many STIs have only mild or no symptoms."

The sexual urge may come with puberty. But the brain can overrule the physical urge by thinking ahead to problems like diseases, untimely pregnancies, and low self-esteem from being thought of as only a sex object.

Abstinence is Popular and Practiced by Millions of People

Although some may try to convince you to engage in premarital sex by telling you that "everyone is doing it," that is not true. Millions of persons successfully practice abstinence.

Youths actually desire an abstinence message. A 2012 survey whose results were published in a lengthy August 2012 report by The National Campaign to Prevent Teen and Unplanned Pregnancy (https://thenationalcampaign.org/sites/default/files/resource-primary-download/wov_2012.pdf)[9] found that 87% of respondents aged 12-19 felt that it was either "very important" or "somewhat important" "for teens to be given a strong message that they should not have sex until they are at least out of high school." The report contains many other findings that you may desire to read, too.

Additionally, a Centers for Disease Control and Prevention study (http://www.cdc.gov/mmwr/preview/mmwrhtml/ss6104a1.htm)[10] covering the reporting period of September 2010-December 2011 found that the majority of students in grades 9-12 had never had sex, finding 52.6% were still virgins. The same study found that only 33.7% of students were "currently sexually active," which they defined as having had sex "during the 3 months before the survey." Even among 12th graders, over half (52.5%) were not "currently sexually active."

In addition to the millions of teens abstaining from premarital sex, a few million persons in their twenties and older probably remain unmarried and virgins. Keeping one's sexual purity is the only method 100% effective at preventing pregnancy and sexually-transmitted diseases.

Dating Without Premarital Sex (or Even Kissing) Has Other Benefits Besides Avoiding Diseases and Unwed Pregnancies

Personally, I consider traditional dating relationships a mistake. Persons spend money on special activities, and focus their time and energy on impressing their dates.

Instead, do a variety of normal activities together. Enjoy common interests together and learn about one another.

Rather than rushing into an emotional, romantic relationship, build a friendship first, and build it slowly. Develop numerous friendships with people with whom one shares common values and interests. Gradually become closer friends with those sharing many common values and interests with you.

Why risk ruining one's future for only a few minutes of sexual pleasure? And how can one evaluate someone from an unbiased perspective when one's emotions are raging out of control?

One of the benefits of practicing sexual abstinence is that abstinence can help persons better develop multidimensional, well-rounded relationships. Ideally, intellectual and spiritual attraction should precede emotional, romantic attraction.

Remaining a virgin until marriage can reduce the likelihood of divorce, too. Several studies indicate that persons who live together before marriage have a higher divorce rate, as mentioned by an article on the HowStuffWorks.com website (http://health.howstuffworks.com/relationships/advice/living-together-before-marriage.htm)[11] and other sources.

Therefore, it is best to resist the temptation to engage in premarital sex. For Christians, I Corinthians 10:13 is a wonderful verse to memorize to bring to mind when faced with temptation. But regardless of one's faith, a key to succeeding at practicing abstinence is to commit to it, then to avoid getting into situations where one may be led to succumb to temptation.

Even if you feel or know premarital sex is wrong, you may be tempted beyond your ability to resist if you get alone in a dark place with someone you care deeply about. Also, remember that both men and women are sensitive to touch. Touching various parts of one another's bodies can lead to arousal.

Kissing is one form of romantic contact that can initiate further arousal that leads to more intimate contact. It is also one way that some diseases are spread. If one has the discipline to do so, I think it is best to avoid the joy of kissing your romantic partner until after the minister states "You may kiss the bride" at the wedding.

I confess though that I didn't always have that view about kissing. I probably would have kissed some girls even in the last two or three years of elementary school if the "right" opportunity presented itself with a few I felt attracted to at different times and places. I probably would have done some other things too, though even by the sixth grade I think I had made a commitment not to get married at least until after college, not to get engaged to be married at least until I was in college, and not to have sex before marriage.

I knew where babies came from and didn't want any before marriage. I also knew in elementary school that I would be meeting new people in high school and college that might be more suitable for me as a spouse than anyone I knew in elementary school. I decided not to commit myself too soon.

During my college years, I did kiss a girl I dated, after asking her permission. And we kissed several times on later dates. But I know now that was a mistake. My views then were not based on Christian beliefs; my views were shaped in large part by television shows I watched as a child, etc.

For example, when I was growing up, watching *The Adventures of Ozzie and Harriet* television show, their son Ricky seemed to think it was okay to kiss a girl on a date. When I watched *The Andy Griffith Show*, Andy seemed to think it was okay for Barney to kiss his date. My views on kissing were based more on those television shows (and others) than on Godly morals.

I feel that those two shows were a bad influence in that particular respect, though I enjoyed watching them as a child.

However, I firmly believe that those two television shows offered far superior morals to a lot of the stuff on television now, so I wonder what young people today think. By the way, although I committed to keeping my pants on and zipped all the time I was dating in college, and God enabled me to keep that commitment, my girlfriend and I did do some things besides kissing that I wouldn't do now if I dated someone. Also, though I never considered us to be going steady, just dating casually, and I told her that I might date others and she could feel free to as well, as far as I know neither of us did date anyone else during that period we dated casually. Now I feel casual dating with kissing, etc., is a mistake and wouldn't do it, if I had it to do over again.

I enjoyed reading Joshua Harris's book *I Kissed Dating Goodbye* (1997; Multnomah Publishers, Inc.; Post Office Box 1720; Sisters, Oregon 97759). It suggests an alternative to the traditional concept of dating that is similar to the one I advocate in several respects. Though the book is written from a Christian perspective, I think much of its basic advice is applicable to all. By the way, a revised edition published after I read it is available. I would love to have read that book years earlier than I did.

Abstinence works. The problem is that abstinence isn't practiced often enough.

We need to do a better job of teaching young people about the physical, emotional, mental, and spiritual problems that are avoided by not engaging in fornication. Compassionate, loving parenting that leads to open communication with teens can help achieve this. Quality religious teachings can help some, too. But school teachers, the media, peers, community leaders, and others need to reinforce the message.

By practicing sexual abstinence before marriage, young men and young women can save themselves for that special someone they intend to share the rest of their lives with. Virginity is a true gift. Keep it until the wedding night as a special gift to share with one's spouse.

Furthermore, do not rush into marriage without knowing your prospective spouse well. Spend time together in a variety of settings and activities. Learn their attitudes regarding money management, careers, having and raising children, spiritual beliefs, morals, etc. Establish and enjoy additional common interests. Know that building a successful lasting relationship requires commitment and shared interests.

After Marriage

Even for a married couple, sexual intercourse is only one of many ways to demonstrate love for each other. Time devoted to sexual love is only a small portion of the 168 hours in a week. In fact, a typical man can only experience an orgasm a few times daily. A woman can experience numerous orgasms daily in various ways, but a woman living a balanced life wouldn't devote her whole day to sexual pleasure, even if her partner were willing to provide her a huge number of orgasms via various methods.

However, through that important sexual component of your marriage, the two of you can make each other very happy, by learning well what makes that one particular special someone happy, during a lifetime of monogamous love for each other, as one significant component of a well-balanced life.

Single for a Lifetime?

Who knows? You may even enjoy remaining single and practicing sexual abstinence throughout your life. Some people may be happier and more productive in God's service this way. In the next chapter, Chapter 28, "Choosing Singleness—A Great Option," I discuss this concept in more detail.

Chapter 27 Questions for Reflection and Discussion
1. What do you support doing to better educate young people on the need to practice sexual abstinence before marriage?

2. How important is the role of parents through their teachings and their examples in the choices their children make regarding sexual purity?
3. What should the government, schools, and society do to promote sexual abstinence?

Chapter 28:
Choosing Singleness—A Great Option

The New Testament cites both Jesus (Matthew 19:10-12) and Paul (I Corinthians 7) as stating it is better to remain single if one has the discipline to do so. For some Christians, it may be the right decision to remain single throughout life. Jesus apparently remained single. Paul apparently was single during his ministry.

However, if a Christian is already married, it is almost always best to remain married unless one's spouse commits adultery or the spouse seeks a divorce. Even when a spouse commits adultery or seeks a divorce, sometimes the marriage can be saved. If a couple experiences major problems in its marriage, prayer, marital counseling, a temporary separation, etc., can often help save the marriage. Also, seeking to resolve minor problems before they escalate into big ones is a key.

But if persons are single when they become Christians, it may be better to remain single and celibate if they have the discipline to do so. Some of the most successful people in history were single. For example, perhaps the Wright brothers would not have been successful in their development of aircraft if they had been married and needed to divide their time between devotion to their family and their work.

Singleness offers an opportunity to dedicate and devote oneself fully to a particular calling or purpose. A single person typically doesn't need to budget as much time for family commitments. Also, a single person doesn't need to consider his or her spouse when contemplating career changes, moves to other locations, or when and where to eat meals.

Typically, I think a single person who does not have responsibilities to a spouse or to children can devote more time to serving God and others. Still, choosing singleness is a personal choice.

For persons deciding to remain single, it is important to develop and maintain a network of friends to fellowship with at least occasionally and to help one another when necessary. Also, remember that singles living alone take total responsibility for their household cleaning, cooking, dishwashing, shopping, laundry, etc. But often singles (including me) live in relatively small apartments rather than large houses, which reduces cleaning duties. Cooking big batches of beans and vegetable soup then refrigerating or freezing leftovers for later saves cooking and dishwashing time, too. And it is easier to shop and do laundry for oneself than for an entire family.

Personally, I think it may be God's calling for me to remain single throughout my life. Furthermore, some of my closest friends remain single.

I enjoy being single. I like being able to cook my own food the way I want it (especially nice since I try to adhere to a vegan diet). In addition, I can make my own decisions about my time and my activities.

Of course, Christians may choose to get married. But I urge Christians to prayerfully consider the impact before getting married. Try to ensure that your relationship with that spouse-to-be will draw you both closer to God's will for your lives if you become a married couple than would be the case if you remained single and celibate.

By seeking God's perfect will, I am confident we will all be happier. For some (including me) that may include remaining single for one's entire life.

If people do get married, there is a high probability that at some point they will become parents. In the next chapter I discuss parenting.

Chapter 28 Questions for Reflection and Discussion
1. Why do you think so few Christians today follow the examples set by Jesus and Paul (and the New Testament teachings) on singleness?
2. Would you encourage young people to seriously consider remaining single throughout their lives if they have the discipline to do so? Why or why not?
3. Do you agree that being single helped Jesus and Paul in their ministries? Why or why not?

Chapter 29:
Parenting

For persons who decide to get married, producing children and becoming parents is often likely to follow. Though I love children, and feel blessed to have two younger sisters, two nephews, and two nieces, I don't feel the desire or ability to be a parent myself with the 24 hours a day, 7 days a week responsibility that comes with it. I am a pro-life Christian who desires no children of my own, so it is a good thing I am single.

Since I have no children and thus am not a parent, I will try to write especially humbly as I provide suggestions about being a true Christian parent. And, of course, although I am not a parent, I was once a child, so I know what it is like to have parents, and can write from a child's perspective even at age 59 (my age in 2017 when I wrote this).

Many books by experts provide lots of pages with detailed instructions on parenting, and I urge parents to consider reading one or more of them. But below I offer some tips of my own on parenting:

- Be truthful. Children need to know they can trust their parents to be truthful with them. I discussed this a bit in Chapter 3: "Be Truthful Always—Avoid Telling 'White Lies.' "
- Seek to agree on how to parent. Children can't do two things at once, so they can't obey contradictory instructions from their parents. I discussed this more in Chapter 20: "What Does It Mean to Honor Your Father and Your Mother?"
- Teach children morals and practice these morals as parents so that children know you value them yourselves. Children need to know right from wrong. The information in this book provides much guidance on what I think moral living entails, but

many topics are not covered that will likely apply to your specific situation and your children.
- Whenever possible explain clearly and logically the reasons for your decisions as parents. "Because I said so" may work when you are around to enforce it, but without a logical reason to back it up, children may not obey in your absence or when they leave home.
- Answer their questions to the extent that it is reasonable, and encourage your children to seek answers from other appropriate sources such as quality reference books, teachers, etc., when you don't know the answer and/or are not available. You don't want your children to turn to peers, poorly written blogs, etc., in their search for answers to important questions.
- Try not to underestimate your children. Children often may know more and think more logically than their parents realize. Children need guidance and education. But that education includes learning to think for themselves. And they need to be trusted when they demonstrate that such trust is warranted, especially as they progress toward the latter teen years.
- Even if your child repeatedly disagrees with you on an issue, remain consistent and firm in a respectful way if you are confident you are right. I remember a few occasions when my mom gave in on certain issues after I repeatedly asked her to change her mind. However, even at that time I sometimes actually wanted her to remain firm on them, and I feel that way even more strongly now.

- Hold them accountable. Children need to be held accountable in a firm but loving way when they knowingly do wrong.
- Make it clear to them that you love them and can be trusted to care for them. Children need that supportive environment.

Please consider my tips in this chapter as only suggestions, not the word of God. But please do prayerfully consider them and apply them to the extent that you find them appropriate for your own circumstances. I hope this chapter is helpful to those of you who are parents, as well as others who interact with children.

One thing parents need to teach their children about is the need to avoid abusing alcoholic beverages. In the next chapter I discuss consuming alcoholic beverages.

Chapter 29 Questions for Reflection and Discussion
1. Do you think it is unreasonable for someone who has never been a parent (like me, the author) to offer advice about parenting? Why or why not?
2. From your childhood, do you remember situations where you feel your parents made mistakes that you learned from that could help you to be a more effective parent yourself?
3. Do you agree with the tips provided in this chapter on parenting? If not, which one(s) do you disagree with and why?
4. What other tips (if any) would you offer?

Chapter 30:
Drinking Alcoholic Beverages Socially in Moderation— Risks Outweigh Benefits

Is it wise for Christians (or anyone) to drink alcoholic beverages socially? Though I personally choose not to drink beer, wine, or other alcoholic beverages, several of my friends do. Often they claim to drink only "moderately." But virtually all of them when questioned admit they have been intoxicated at least once. Since many of us (blush!) have trouble eating just one potato chip, cookie, etc.—why take a chance with liquor?

Furthermore, virtually everyone I know who consumes alcoholic beverages began doing so before reaching the Kentucky minimum legal drinking age of 21. Therefore, most broke the law in two ways: by drinking underage and by getting drunk.

Why do persons consume alcoholic beverages? After all, the risks from socially drinking even one alcoholic beverage far outweigh the benefits for the average person in my view (and in the view of many others).

Consumption of alcoholic beverages impairs judgment and contributes to a huge number of automobile accidents, other types of accidents, diseases, and violence. Furthermore: "Impairment due to alcohol use begins to occur at levels well below the legal limit" for blood alcohol content (BAC) according to the Centers for Disease Control and Prevention (http://www.cdc.gov/alcohol/faqs.htm).[12]

Even one drink of an alcoholic beverage has some harmful effects. "Some skills are significantly impaired at 0.01 percent BAC" according to information on the National Institute on Alcohol Abuse and Alcoholism's website (http://pubs.niaaa.nih.gov/publications/aa52.htm).[13] Drinking less than one beer would lead to a larger BAC than 0.01!

My Personal Experience
I am thankful that I did not have easy access to alcoholic beverages

when I was a boy. I lived most of my childhood in counties where the sale of alcoholic beverages was illegal. Neither my parents nor my friends consumed them to my knowledge, and I didn't know who the bootleggers were or where the stills were. In addition, I didn't see people drinking in my neighborhood, though some probably did—alcoholic beverages were sold legally in nearby areas.

Limited access is probably the main reason I did not indulge my curiosity as a boy and try out alcohol in response to the widespread advertising for beer and other alcoholic beverages on television, radio, and in the print media. I also saw alcohol consumption on television shows and in movies. But I rarely saw it in person.

By the time I started college, I had decided to abstain from alcoholic beverages unless needed for medicinal reasons. I think I made my decision by the seventh or eighth grade actually. If I remember correctly, my final decision came after seeing a video in an eighth grade class that claimed each serving of an alcoholic beverage killed 10,000 brain cells. I don't know if that figure is accurate, but it stuck with me and contributed toward keeping me from trying out alcoholic beverages. I didn't know how many brain cells I had, but I didn't want to lose any of them.

College classmates who overindulged and vomited, injured themselves physically while intoxicated, lacked memory of what they did the day before, etc., reinforced this decision to abstain. I could have fun watching college sporting events and engaging in other activities without consuming an intoxicating drink.

I was (and still am) blessed to have several friends who enjoy fun activities without indulging in alcohol consumption. Seeking out persons who also avoid drinking alcoholic beverages helps one remain steadfast in one's decision.

Does Drinking in Moderation Offer Any Health Benefits?

Some researchers claim that drinking alcohol in moderation provides health benefits through reducing the risk of heart disease, etc. However, the American Heart Association on its website (http://www.heart.org/HEARTORG/Conditions/More/MyHeartand StrokeNews/Alcohol-and-Heart-Disease_UCM_305173_Article.jsp)[14] advises nondrinkers "NOT to start drinking." It also urges pregnant women to abstain totally.

The risks from consuming alcoholic beverages casually almost always outweigh the benefits. Furthermore, some research indicates that grape juice provides some of the same benefits as moderate alcohol consumption without the harmful effects and risks of alcohol, as reported on MayoClinic.com (http://www.mayoclinic.com/health/food-and-nutrition/AN00576),[15] among other sources.

And many, including some scientists, question whether alcohol really is beneficial in moderation. One of the sources that discusses this in more detail is a June 16, 2009 *New York Times* piece on the *New York Times* website, titled "Alcohol's Good for You? Some Scientists Doubt It" (http://query.nytimes.com/gst/fullpage.html?res=9D05EFD81F3BF935A25755C0A96F9C8B63&sec=&spon=&pagewanted=1).[16]

Please do not succumb to the false and misleading advertising for alcoholic beverages. In fact, it would be great if people would unite to stop such advertising. The American Medical Association has opposed advertising for "alcoholic beverages except for inside retail or wholesale outlets" (https://www.ama-assn.org/ssl3/ecomm/PolicyFinderForm.pl?site=www.ama-assn.org&uri=/resources/html/PolicyFinder/policyfiles/HnE/H-30.940.HTM).[17]

I agree with the American Medical Association. Let's stop allowing advertising for beer and other alcoholic beverages via mass media sources like television, radio, magazines, newspapers, online, and in similar ways.

Some persons claim that they drink to relax, to enjoy themselves, or to forget about their problems. Surely they can find an alternative way to relax and enjoy themselves! If people have problems, they can seek solutions. Retreating from problems into alcohol will not solve them, and in many cases will make them worse. Since I am not a doctor, I can't give medical advice, but I think the dangers of consuming alcoholic beverages socially outweigh any benefits.

Furthermore, as I stated earlier, persons I know who claim to only drink alcoholic beverages in moderation almost invariably admit to having been legally drunk at least once in the past. The best way to avoid becoming drunk drinking alcoholic beverages is to never drink alcoholic beverages.

Health Problems Associated With Alcohol Abuse

The health problems associated with alcohol abuse are numerous and (in many cases) well documented. The lengthy quote from the Centers for Disease Control and Prevention website (http://www.cdc.gov/alcohol/faqs.htm)[18] below summarizes several of them:

> "Excessive drinking both in the form of heavy drinking or binge drinking, is associated with numerous health problems, including—
>
> Chronic diseases such as liver cirrhosis (damage to liver cells); pancreatitis (inflammation of the pancreas); various cancers, including liver, mouth, throat, larynx (the voice box), and esophagus; high blood pressure; and psychological disorders.
>
> Unintentional injuries, such as motor-vehicle traffic crashes, falls, drowning, burns and firearm injuries.
>
> Violence, such as child maltreatment, homicide, and suicide.
>
> Harm to a developing fetus if a woman drinks while pregnant, such as fetal alcohol spectrum disorders.

Sudden infant death syndrome (SIDS)." (Source for above quote: http://www.cdc.gov/alcohol/faqs.htm)[18]

A study published in 2009 in the British medical journal *The Lancet* indicated that approximately "one in 25 deaths worldwide are attributable to alcohol," as stated on the Lancet's website (http://www.thelancet.com/series/alcohol-and-global-health)[19] and reported in numerous news articles.

And the United States legal blood alcohol limit of 0.08 percent for driving is not as strict as that of many other countries, as noted by DrinkDriving.org (http://www.drinkdriving.org/worldwide_drink_driving_limits.php)[20] and numerous other sources.

You may locate numerous resources discussing various harmful effects of consuming alcoholic beverages if you so desire. Information is available online, in libraries, and in bookstores.

A Few Recommendations

Despite alcohol's harmful effects, due to the millions of people in the United States who already consume alcohol (many supposedly in moderation), prohibition is not practical at this time. Prohibition was tried several decades ago; enforcement was not effective. Instead, I advocate eliminating (or severely restricting) advertising for this harmful product as a step toward reducing its widespread abuse.

If we help current alcohol abusers deal with their addictions and prevent young people from taking their first drink of beer, wine, whiskey, or any other alcoholic beverage, maybe in a generation or two we can virtually eliminate alcohol abuse. In the United States, enforcing the U.S. minimum legal age of 21 for starting to drink and the U.S. legal blood alcohol limit of .08 percent are keys.

Alcohol is still used in certain medications. But alternative medicines without alcohol exist for most medicinal needs now. Therefore, alcohol is less useful for medicinal purposes than centuries ago. Like penicillin or any other medicine, alcohol ought not to be consumed unless needed—and only consumed in the proper dosage. Alcohol-free medications often are more effective than those containing alcohol and frequently have the additional benefit of producing fewer harmful side effects. In fact, the instructions for numerous medicines specifically state to avoid consuming alcohol while taking the medication.

In this chapter I focused on logical, secular reasons for avoiding social drinking of alcoholic beverages. But persons seeking a scriptural reference can turn to Proverbs 31:4-7, which urges kings not to drink wine. Readers can also turn to the various Bible passages that discuss alcohol abuse and drunkenness, as well as passages about certain persons who abstained from wine and strong drink, such as Daniel and John the Baptist.

Eliminating (or even greatly reducing) alcohol abuse won't be easy. But the combined loving efforts of parents, educators, community leaders, and law enforcement officials, along with restrictions on advertising, can go a long way toward achieving this. Do you agree it is a worthwhile goal? I hope so! I urge you to seek to relax and enjoy safe fun without alcoholic beverages!

Just as abstaining from social drinking of alcoholic beverages is wise, it is also wise to be careful about which other drinks—and which foods—we choose to consume. In the next chapter I discuss some benefits of a vegan diet.

Chapter 30 Questions for Reflection and Discussion
1. What is your attitude toward the consumption of alcoholic beverages?
2. If you consume alcoholic beverages, did you start drinking them before you reached legal age?
3. If you have ever been intoxicated, what advice would you give others about intoxication?

Chapter 31:
Reducing One's Food Budget (And Other Benefits of a Vegan Diet)

It is important for Christians (all persons really) to manage money wisely. Food is perhaps the most important item in the typical person's budget. We all eat, don't we?

If you take the Bible literally, humans and animals were originally vegans, as stated in Genesis 1:29, 30. Even without the words from the Bible though, logical reasons exist to eat a vegan diet.

A vegan diet can be healthier for us than one loaded with meat and dairy products, in addition to being better for the animals. A key additional benefit of a vegan diet is that it can be cheaper than one based on meat and dairy products. In many cases, plant-based foods that are good for our health are much cheaper than those derived from animals. I try to basically adhere to a vegan diet, and my grocery spending often averages under $5 a day. Yes, persons can eat a healthy vegan diet for less than $5 a day—at least in most places in the U.S.

Most of us can substantially reduce the amount of money we spend on food. Below I list five steps that can help most persons eat healthier and reduce their food budgets substantially.

Five Steps to Help Most Persons Eat Healthier and Cheaper

The first step (I think you guessed this one was coming!) is to reduce or eliminate eating at restaurants. Restaurant food is typically much more expensive than food bought at a grocery and often is loaded with additives you don't want. I rarely eat out.

Second, substitute beans for most of your meat purchases. Pinto beans and whole grain cornbread (or whole grain brown rice) provide an excellent source of protein and amino acids. Purchase numerous other types of beans to add variety—great northern beans, black beans, kidney beans, red beans, cranberry beans, lima beans, navy beans, etc. I often prepare a big pot of beans and refrigerate leftovers for the following days. They can also be frozen, but since I only have the compartment above my refrigerator for frozen items, I seldom use my limited frozen food space for this.

Third, eat a variety of whole grains instead of consuming refined white flour. The choices include whole grain cornmeal, whole grain wheat flour, and whole grain brown rice, as well as numerous other grains. My favorites include white whole wheat flour and whole grain yellow cornmeal. Though whole grains may be a bit more expensive per serving than refined grains, they are still relatively cheap compared to most other foods. Also, whole grains fill you up better than refined grains, so you eat less. I frequently bake a pan of corn muffins and refrigerate leftovers to eat later.

Fourth, eat a serving or two of nuts and/or seeds daily. These provide nutritional value and cholesterol-free fat. This fat is good for us compared to the more saturated fat in meat. Eating a serving or two of peanuts, almonds, sunflower seeds, walnuts, and/or other types of nuts and/or seeds daily provides part of a well-balanced diet. Most days I enjoy a serving of almonds as well as a serving of peanuts or some other type of nuts and/or seeds. By the way, technically peanuts are a legume, not a nut.

Fifth, eat several servings of fruits and vegetables daily. On a per-serving basis even fresh fruits and vegetables are not very expensive. Fresh fruits can average less than 40 cents per serving here in Kentucky, and vegetables can average less than 20 cents per serving. Therefore, less than $2.50 per day can pay for a person's daily allotment of fruits and vegetables (three servings of fruits and five servings of vegetables). If you grow your own vegetables and are blessed with fruit trees in your yard, you can save much more on the costs of your fruits and vegetables—and eat better quality ones, too. But that isn't very realistic for persons (like me) who live in an apartment. The prices per serving I listed above are for those of us who buy our fruits and vegetables at supermarkets (on sale).

Bananas are often the cheapest fruit. For example, if it takes 2 ½ bananas to weigh a pound, at 55 cents per pound bananas would cost 22 cents each. Apples are closer to 40 cents per serving. Whichever fruits are on sale this week at the local supermarket are probably about 40 cents per serving or less. The key is buying fruits (and vegetables) when they are on sale. Since the sale items vary each week, over time this adds nice variety to one's diet.

Some vegetables are relatively cheap per serving (cabbage, carrots, celery, corn, onions, potatoes, etc.), but others are relatively expensive (asparagus, spinach, etc.). However, the average cost can work out to less than 20 cents per serving. If you have extra freezer space, buying lots of frozen vegetables on sale (or freezing your own) can cut costs.

Omega-3 Fatty Acids

Many nutritionists recommend eating fish for the Omega-3 fatty acids it contains. Since I am trying to adhere to a vegan diet, I try to avoid eating fish.

Therefore, I use ground flaxseeds as an alternative to fish for the fatty acids. I often sprinkle some ground flaxseeds on my breakfast cereal, biscuits, or pancakes to get a vegan source of Omega-3 fatty acids; walnuts are another good source of Omega-3s. Since cooking apparently damages the Omega-3 fatty acids in the ground flaxseeds, I apply the flaxseeds after preparing oatmeal, biscuits, pancakes, wheat farina, etc.

Microalgae are another vegan source of Omega-3 fatty acids; microalgae contains DHA and EPA Omega-3 fatty acids, making their fatty acids more similar to those in fish than the ALA in ground flaxseeds. It is probably best to consume both flaxseeds and microalgae in your diet.

Next I will discuss possible menu items for daily meals.

Breakfast

Breakfast can be the cheapest meal. Oatmeal, wheat farina, homemade biscuits and gravy, pancakes, cereal and soymilk (with cereal bought on sale), etc., are all relatively cheap.

I also usually include a piece of fresh fruit or juice in my breakfast—sometimes both. I drink a glass of orange juice most days. I buy twelve-ounce containers of frozen orange juice concentrate enriched with calcium, which cost about $1.50-$1.75 for store brands. The frozen concentrate makes six servings of eight ounces each, for a cost of less than 30 cents per serving. Even with my limited freezer space, I try to keep about four containers of frozen juice concentrate on hand.

Lunch at Work or Other Meals Away from Home

As a freelance writer, I am often home for my meals. Also, I am blessed to be able to walk home for lunch from work at my second job (a short three-minute walk). But if you must eat a meal away from home, such as a lunch at work, consider packing a meal, such as a sandwich, fruit, and a salad. Some type of whole wheat bread is usually available in a supermarket on sale for about $2 a loaf or less.

Brown bagging your own peanut butter and jelly sandwich(es), banana(s), and a salad will almost certainly be cheaper than eating in a restaurant and likely more nutritious, too. If your workplace lacks a refrigerator, you can pack the salad in an airtight plastic container with some ice cubes to keep it cold. I did that a few times when I worked farther away, and I didn't have easy access to a refrigerator. If you are concerned someone may tamper with your lunch during the few hours before you eat it, try to put it in a locker, your locked car, or some other safe place.

Also, be sensitive to the allergies of others. For example, many have allergies to peanuts. Your school or workplace may prohibit peanuts (and peanut products like peanut butter sandwiches) for this reason. Even if they aren't prohibited where you go to school or work, please eat them responsibly.

Snacks

For snacking, popcorn prepared on the stove without adding salt or much cooking oil provides fiber, some nutrition, and relatively few calories. If you can air pop it, even better. Popcorn prepared this way is cheaper—and better for one's health—than potato chips!

Fresh fruits and vegetables can also be tasty and nutritious snacks, with or without a nutritious dip. Homemade treats like oatmeal cookies and banana nut bread can be delicious, too, and relatively low in sugar and fat. I usually substitute applesauce or molasses for the sugar in recipes, which adds nutrition without increasing the cost much.

Dinner, Supper, and Other Home-Cooked Meals

Preparing some type of beans and some type of whole grain bread provides a tasty, nutritious entree for the main meal of the day. A variety of spices and seasonings can add flavor. There are numerous recipes available online and in cookbooks, in addition to the basic ones on the bags of beans and grains.

For vegetable side dishes, one choice is to add a variety of fresh vegetables chosen from those purchased on sale this week and those still on hand from previous weeks' purchases. I also frequently prepare a big pot of vegetable soup and enjoy leftovers later. And I often microwave a bag of frozen mixed vegetables, stir fry vegetables, or other frozen vegetables. I also keep a supply of canned vegetables on hand.

Fresh fruit can be dessert. In addition to apples and bananas, each week some fruit is usually on sale locally (such as apricots, blackberries, blueberries, cantaloupes, grapefruits, grapes, peaches, pears, pineapples, plums, raspberries, strawberries, watermelons, etc.).

If you prefer, you can prepare some type of homemade treat for dessert. Homemade cakes, pies, cookies, candies, etc., are usually fairly cheap per serving. But it is usually best to limit one's intake of these—they often have lots of fat, sugar, salt, and calories, even when they are homemade. However, numerous vegan recipes with limited fat, sugar, and salt content are available online that make such "junk food" a bit healthier eating for us.

When time permits, I enjoy baking homemade cinnamon-oatmeal-raisin cookies, using molasses or applesauce to sweeten them. They are tasty, somewhat nutritious, and relatively low in fat—I use little vegetable oil in them.

Additional Information

To save time, I often prepare food in big batches even though I live alone. I can refrigerate (or freeze) leftovers to microwave later for a quick meal. This works well for many foods, such as the beans and vegetable soup I mentioned earlier.

I try to eat a proper diet. But neither I nor anyone else eats perfectly, so I recommend taking a daily multivitamin. I typically take one with my first meal of the day. For less than 15 cents per day, $15 for a bottle of 100 vitamins, you can add a quality multivitamin to your daily diet. I confess that the brands I currently buy are probably not vegan vitamins. But I am confident that there are some quality vegan multivitamins available, and I hope to find one.

For those on vegan diets, B12 is one of the difficult vitamins to get in one's diet. I use soymilk enriched with vitamin B12 and calcium, as well as occasionally eating breakfast cereal enriched with B12. A well-balanced vegan diet meets most other nutritional needs. For those of you not on a vegan diet, buying cows' milk instead of soymilk will probably reduce your milk costs by about 50%, since soymilk is about twice as expensive as cows' milk where I shop—though I admit that I personally feel cows' milk should be reserved for calves.

Omega-3 fatty acids are another nutrient difficult to get from a vegan diet. If you haven't already, please read the section earlier in this chapter where I discussed vegan sources for Omega-3 fatty acids.

One way to save money is by using manufacturers' coupons and store coupons regularly. I use such coupons occasionally. But coupon use is not a big factor in my food budget. It seems that coupons typically are not available for fresh fruits and vegetables, whole grains, dry beans, and store brands, which are the major parts of my food budget.

I am not a medical professional or a dietician, so I can't give medical advice or professional nutritional advice. But I think persons who follow my suggestions with modifications for their personal calorie and nutrition needs will enjoy a better diet than the typical person eats—at a much lower cost.

I urge you to seek out more information, too. Much helpful specific diet information is available on the United States government websites Health.gov (http://www.health.gov/dietaryguidelines/)[21] and ChooseMyPlate.gov (http://www.choosemyplate.gov/).[22]

If you desire a more specific plan for reducing your food budget, the U.S. Department of Agriculture provides a detailed list of specific quantities and types of foods necessary daily and weekly to prepare well-balanced meals at home very economically, in its Thrifty Food Plan, 2006 (http://www.cnpp.usda.gov/sites/default/files/usda_food_plans_cost_of_food/TFP2006Report.pdf).[23] Another U.S. Department of Agriculture webpage provides an updated cost for the items in the Thrifty Food Plan, 2006, as of April 2019 (https://fns-prod.azureedge.net/sites/default/files/resource-files/CostofFoodApr2019.pdf).[24] The food costs for the average adult under their "Thrifty plan" are between $5 and $6 daily for most adults. Prices do change frequently. You can probably find more up-to-date data on the U.S. Department of Agriculture website by the time you read this. By the way, I did not use their "Thrifty plan" data in compiling my own plan. Since I omit meat (due to seeking to adhere to a vegan diet) my plan is a bit cheaper—about $5 daily.

Yes, you can eat a very healthy diet cheaply!

Finally, most of us eat a wide variety of foods and don't always choose the right ones or prepare them properly. In the next chapter, I briefly discuss the "miracle" of how the human digestive system and the human immune system protect our bodies.

Chapter 31 Questions for Reflection and Discussion
1. How much of your food budget goes toward restaurant meals? Would you like to cut your food costs by reducing the number of times you eat out?
2. Since beans and whole grains are low in fat and cheaper than meat, are you willing to cut back (or eliminate) meat consumption? Why or why not?
3. How hard is it to resist the temptation to feast on snacks or desserts high in fat, sugar, and/or salt?

Chapter 32:
The "Miracle" of the Digestive System and the Immune System

One key to living a successful true Christian life is to take good care of our human body's digestive system and our immune system.

The ways that the human digestive system works and the ways that the human immune system works astound me. I don't claim to understand them.

It is almost unbelievable to me that a human being can intake such a wide variety of foods and drinks and somehow the body usually seems to convert much of this material into usable energy and typically seems to eliminate most unneeded portions through restroom trips, etc. Similarly, it is amazing how the human body can be exposed to such a huge variety of bacteria, etc., and our immune system seems to usually protect us from most of them.

I lack the knowledge and wisdom to explain it, and this brief chapter likely wouldn't allow the space to do so anyway. However, there are some things we humans can do to help out our digestive and immune systems.

Eating a well-balanced, nutritious vegan diet as I discussed in the previous chapter is one. The digestive system functions better with the right foods and drinks than it does with the wrong ones. Avoiding overeating is another key.

Regarding our immune system, though it can protect us from much, we help it by washing our hands regularly, avoiding putting our dirty hands in our mouths, etc., and by limiting our exposure to contagious diseases when reasonably possible. Also, try to avoid eating and drinking after others.

But even as we try to do our best, we need to trust God for the rest. Also, sometimes it seems as if our immune system is improved by not going to extremes in our efforts to be clean. Somehow God (and our moms) nourished and protected us in the womb, and somehow we are protected on a daily basis, maybe by God answering prayers.

I remember as a child playing with raw sewage from a straight line pipe into a creek, using my fingers to move around the mercury from a broken thermometer, and engaging in other risky behaviors that I would not desire to do now. At least sometimes I ate food with my fingers with unwashed hands.

Somehow God protected me then though, as God often seems to protect us despite our errors. But I think as we progress in our knowledge and wisdom through the grace of God, we increase our chances of doing what is best for our digestive system, our immune system, and the rest of our body.

As you seek to take better care of your digestive and immune systems, as well as the rest of your body, you may find that one key to good health is having fun. In the next chapter I discuss some free and cheap ways to have fun.

Chapter 32 Questions for Reflection and Discussion
1. What are your views about the "miracle" of how the human digestive system works?
2. What do you think about eating a healthy diet? If you feel the need to eat better, are you willing and able to take steps to eat more healthily?
3. Do you think the way that the human immune system works is a "miracle"? Why or why not?
4. To what extent do you think we need to protect ourselves from bacteria, chemicals, etc., by washing regularly and taking other precautions?

Chapter 33:
Free and Cheap Ways to Have Fun

Christians (and others) can enjoy loads of fun cheaply. Several of the most enjoyable experiences of my life cost nothing or were very inexpensive. Free and cheap ways to have fun abound. Many even benefit others.

And I feel true Christians will seek to be good stewards of their money by not spending extravagantly on leisure activities if suitable cheaper alternatives exist. Below I discuss some cheap ways to have fun.

Games

One of my favorite cheap ways to have fun is playing games of various types. Since the next chapter deals with what I call old-fashioned games, I will not discuss them in detail here. But board and card games can be loads of fun. Numerous enjoyable outdoor games exist, too. However, lots of alternatives to games exist for fun and economical entertainment. Please read on.

Libraries

I have loved to read and write since I was a child. Visiting the library to skim or read magazines and newspapers and to check out books is a joy. Many public libraries now have DVDs, music CDs, books on tape, ebooks, etc., to check out for free, in addition to printed materials.

Computers are often available at libraries for public use to do online research, surf the Internet, play video games, etc. Libraries also often offer a variety of programs. For example, my local library (the Lexington, Kentucky Public Library) offers numerous activities for children and contains a theater that periodically shows movies and documentaries, as well as hosting seminars and discussions on various topics. Free computer classes and classes on other subjects are also offered at the Lexington Public Library.

For inexpensive entertainment, a local library is great! You can probably even research online at your library about inexpensive fun things to do—or check out a book on the subject!

Various Activities for Cities, College Towns, and Rural Areas

Cities and college towns often offer a variety of free activities, including seminars, lectures, concerts, athletic events, etc. Rural areas often offer wonderful opportunities to farm/garden, hike, observe wildlife, enjoy the beauty of nature, etc. I've enjoyed hiking in rural areas in southeastern Kentucky, as well as attending a variety of events here in the central Kentucky city of Lexington. I do feel especially blessed here in Lexington, since the city is a college town that offers a lot of cultural activities and the city government also wisely took steps to preserve much of the city's greenspace.

Visiting a local park can be lots of fun. I may always be a kid at heart—I think I sometimes feel 19 years old (or maybe even 9!) instead of 59. It's sometimes hard for me to believe I turned 59 in 2017. Even as an adult I think I would still enjoy occasionally swinging on a swing and sliding down a slide that will accommodate adults. Please do read and adhere to age restrictions on the equipment though.

Larger parks often feature lengthy hiking trails, swimming pools, tennis courts, volleyball courts, basketball courts, and fields for playing baseball, softball, and soccer. Hiking is one of my favorite activities.

Taking a nature hike can be lots of fun whether walking in your neighborhood, at an arboretum, on a nearby hillside, in a valley, or on a field. The variety of plants, insects, animals, birds, etc., that one can see even in urban areas is amazing. Gathering walnuts, raspberries, blackberries, cherries, pawpaws, and other nuts and fruits in season (in areas where such picking of fruits and nuts is legal) adds to the fun—watch for snakes though and be aware of chemical spraying in many areas. Government road crews often spray plants near roads with chemicals (to kill weeds) that may get on or even into the edible fruits and nuts. Utility crews may also spray near such things as electric power lines and natural gas lines. Please avoid eating nuts and fruits from plants that have been sprayed this way.

A bicycle ride can be a nice alternative to a hike. You can cover more territory in the same amount of time, since bicyclists typically go faster than hikers. If your bicycle is equipped with bike racks, you can transport more things, too, than on a hiker's backpack. Bicyclists also have the option of dismounting and hiking to particular destinations on foot.

Whether walking or biking, take appropriate items for the trip. Some items to consider taking include a jacket, coat, hood or toboggan, gloves, flashlights, reflectors, wide-brimmed hat or sunscreen, bicycle helmet, raincoat, extra pair of dry socks in a waterproof bag, water, food, maps, phone, emergency phone numbers, etc. Also, pace yourself to avoid overexertion.

Visiting museums, zoos, historic homes, and other facilities can be both entertaining and educational. Many offer free admission or reduced prices on certain days or at certain times.

On a hot summer day, a friendly water gun fight can be thrilling. Old plastic dishwashing liquid spray bottles that have been rinsed out can suffice as squirt guns if you don't desire to buy one of the numerous varieties of toy ones.

Gardening can be fun for children and adults, whether it involves one plant or several. Planting a few seeds in a pot or the ground, watering them, and watching how they grow and produce flowers, vegetables, herbs, etc., can be a joy. Vegetable gardening can even be economical; it can provide nutritious, quality fresh food at very reasonable costs. Living on a farm enables even more planting—as well as the opportunity to produce much excess for sale and/or gifts to others.

In the spring of 2013 I planted some basil seeds and parsley seeds in pots outside my apartment. They grew and prospered, producing tasty basil and parsley. Obviously, I am not a big scale gardener. But many years ago I grew a rose bush, other flowers, tomato plants, bell peppers, strawberries, cabbage, carrots, etc., at various times when I lived at other locations.

Just Fellowshipping

Just fellowshipping with others can be fun, depending on the situation and the individual(s) involved. With some people, it is a joy just conversing: sharing personal stories, discussing current events, and telling jokes. It's important to be with the right people though, rather than with people who use idle time for illegal or immoral purposes.

Volunteering

Also, volunteering for a local organization can be lots of fun, in addition to helping others. Serving meals at soup kitchens, visiting nursing homes, and tutoring people are a few of the many ways volunteers can help others, develop new friends, and get a good deal of satisfaction. My volunteer efforts have been somewhat limited. But I have helped: (1) as a member of a Christian singles group serving meals at a soup kitchen, (2) as a member of a Christian singles Sunday School class helping at a local food bank, (3) at an organization that donates educational books overseas, (4) pick up litter in my neighborhood, (5) in a very small way as one of many volunteers helping with preparations for a Friends of the Library book sale, and (6) on several other things over the years. But most of my volunteer efforts have either been while playing a very small role as part of a group organized and led by others or been relatively minor individual efforts—virtually all of them done for a short period of time. Still, I have been blessed immeasurably in my minor roles and feel that as I do more I can and will be blessed much more. I think that is true for you as well. If I can do it, I think most others can, too. Over the years I've enjoyed helping various friends, neighbors, and acquaintances, as well as strangers. By the way, I believe that the best volunteer work is frequently done anonymously without anyone else except God and the person doing it knowing.

Summary

Yes, for very little cost, I've enjoyed lots of hours playing games with relatives and friends, hiking, fighting with squirt guns, reading, attending seminars and lectures, doing some volunteer work, bicycling, and visiting museums and other facilities. Maybe you can enjoy cheap fun, too!

One of the best free or cheap ways to have fun may be playing games. In the next chapter I focus on playing games.

Chapter 33 Questions for Reflection and Discussion
1. What free or cheap fun things to do can you think of to add to the list in the chapter?
2. What are your favorite ways to spend your free time? Are they relatively inexpensive? If not, are there cheaper alternatives you would enjoy as much?
3. How often do you visit your local library? How often do you attend various free events in your area?
4. Are you active in some type of volunteer work? If not, why not?

Chapter 34:
Playing Games—Old Fashioned Fun

Christians (including me) and others often have more fun playing old fashioned games than playing with the expensive new high-tech entertainment options widely available now. Buying a few games instead of spending lots of money on more expensive entertainment options is wise as I see it. Too many Christians (and others) blow their budgets on expensive entertainment luxuries. Even frequent trips to a movie theater add up to a big expense quickly.

As a child during the 1960s and 1970s I loved to play games—I still do when time permits. Perhaps almost everyone finds playing games fun to some extent!

I enjoyed board games and card games, as well as outdoor games like tag, croquet, and badminton. They provided fun, cheap entertainment that I often enjoyed even more than some more expensive things my family did, like taking regular trips to the theater.

Many of the games I've enjoyed have been played for centuries, such as checkers and chess. But numerous others were either trademarked games or trademarked versions of old games.

Persons can have hours of fun with just a few favorite games. In fact a few favorites got most of my playing time even though I was blessed to get the opportunity to play a wide variety of games.

I remember happily spending many hours with friends playing the Parker Brothers board game Monopoly® on hot summer afternoons. When my mom was caught up on her housework she would often join us for a game, which added to the fun. Monopoly® became my favorite board or card game for 5 or more persons.

My dad often joined in to play games of the Parker Brothers card game Rook® after work and on weekends when one of my friends was over. Rook® was especially enjoyable with four players, with two persons playing as partners. Often mom and I would partner together and dad (who was the best player) would team up with one of my neighborhood friends. Rook® became my favorite four-person board or card game.

On summer evenings after it cooled down, frequently a group of us would play croquet out in the grass. We also threw Frisbees,® played tag, and enjoyed other outdoor games. In southeastern Kentucky (where I lived during my childhood), there was usually a relatively lengthy period of shady daylight in the low-lying areas after the sun went behind the mountaintops in the early evening.

While we were in study hall in high school, my best friend taught me how to play the card game rummy. (Yes, we frequently studied, too!) We had lots of fun playing rummy.

I experienced much fun and fellowship playing games as a child, as well as during my college years—and still do as an adult. When I was in college, I often purchased a game as a Christmas gift to take home for the younger of my two sisters. We spent many happy hours together playing various games during my visits from college.

While the focus when I played games was on fun and fellowship (and I enjoyed it when I won, too), some games were educational. For example, I improved my vocabulary and spelling by playing Scrabble®; playing Monopoly® probably increased my math skills.

As if playing games at home wasn't enough, playing peg games on tables in restaurants was a fun way to pass time while waiting for food (or for others to finish eating) on a few occasions when our family took a vacation trip to the southeastern United States (further southeast for those who think Kentucky where I live is in the southeast). I've since seen the games in Kentucky, too.

Games were also a part of our car trips. While dad drove our family to visit relatives (and also on Sunday afternoon drives around the area where we lived), the family frequently played a game to see who could spot the most Volkswagen Beetles, which were then popular. The first person to see one would say "I see one." We kept count to see who said "I see one" first the most.

Improving Communication

I think persons can talk to each other while playing old fashioned games more easily than while playing fast-paced video games or while watching a movie or television show. Much conversation took place as I played games with relatives and friends. We discussed a variety of topics.

I did not hear about the discussion game, The Ungame,® until long after I became an adult. But it seems to be a wonderful way to get to know friends and family better. I love the noncompetitive concept behind it and its emphasis on improving communication between people. Trivial Pursuit® and Pictionary® also can generate better communication, as well as broadening everyone's horizons in certain ways, but I don't feel they come close to achieving the type of openness, trust, and increase in knowledge about one another that can ideally be obtained through The Ungame® when it is played honestly by people who share a reasonable amount of trust for one another. I actually thought of creating a game along the lines of The Ungame® before I found it. And since it basically consists of a deck of cards, it is relatively cheap and portable. I highly recommend The Ungame® as a tool to try out for improving communication between people.

Concluding Thoughts on Games

Though I played a wide variety of games, a few favorites like Monopoly,® Rook,® Scrabble,® rummy, and croquet seemed to get the majority of my game-playing time during my childhood. If I had known about The Ungame® then, I like to think it would have been added to that list of favorites. I highly recommend it.

It's not necessary to buy a lot of games or to spend a lot of money on them. I rarely got tired of just playing Rook.® But you could purchase all the games listed in the previous paragraph (except croquet) for a total of well under $50, when you find them on sale. One family trip to the theater could cost more than $50, including popcorn and soft drinks. And the Christian fellowship with family and friends would likely be lacking in the theater.

Of course, it is important to keep games in proper perspective. Doing other fun activities, volunteering, studying, and working are all an important part of a balanced life. However, happily playing various games with friends and relatives has definitely been a joyous part of my life. Yes, enjoyable and memorable.

One activity Christians would do well to undertake besides playing games is preparing for a potential emergency situation. In the next chapter I discuss emergency preparedness.

Chapter 34 Questions for Reflection and Discussion
1. What types of games do you, your family, and your friends enjoy playing? Are they inexpensive?
2. How often does your family have a game night or game afternoon when you play board or card games (or other games) and enjoy fellowship together?
3. Have you played the discussion game The Ungame®? Will you after reading this chapter?

Chapter 35:
Emergency Preparedness Kit Setup and Preparing for a Disaster

God can protect us from disasters. But I am confident God wants us to do our part to prepare for potential disasters, too.

If an emergency causes your home to lose electrical power, phone service, and safe tap water, what can you do? What if the emergency also makes your local roads unsafe due to downed power lines and trees?

One key is preparing in advance. Your survival may depend on it. One step in this preparation is assembling an emergency kit.

What to Include in Your Emergency Kit

Keeping a supply of essential items on hand is important. Two important things to have are water and food.

Water: I normally keep about seven 24 packs of ½ liter containers of bottled water on hand and replace it about every two years (the recommended shelf life on the bottles). That water could last me three weeks if I use about one gallon per day. I am single and live alone. Add additional quantities if your household contains more than one person.

Do you think you lack adequate space for this? If so, you are probably wrong. Since I fit it in my studio efficiency apartment of less than 300 square feet, I think most others (in the U.S. at least) can, too.

Food: Unless you have alternative means to cook food (and wash utensils) when your electrical power and natural gas and water are off, I urge you to stock only prepared food and disposable eating utensils for emergencies. This means foods like canned vegetables, canned and dried fruits, nuts, dry cereals that are ready to eat, crackers, etc. Keep a manual can opener on hand for use when electrical power is unavailable, too.

Other items to include in your survival kits are flashlights, a battery-powered radio, batteries, a First Aid kit, any medications you need, and suitable clothing. For a more complete list, I recommend consulting a U.S. government website, FEMA.gov, (https://www.fema.gov/media-library-data/1e04d512b273e2133cb865833cc0e32d/FEMA_checklist_parent_508_071513.pdf)[25] which provides an "Emergency Supplies List" of items to keep on hand for "your family's emergency kit." Their list provides excellent advice as a starting point on what to include in an emergency kit. You may desire additional items not on their list, too, for your personal situation.

Both FEMA.gov and the Ready.gov (https://www.ready.gov/)[26] website provide much more information about disaster preparedness you may want to read.

Keep at Least a Three Week Supply of Essentials

Both federal government websites listed in the preceding section of this chapter recommend keeping at least a three days' supply of water, food, and other items. However, I recommend a three week supply (or more) of food, water, medicine, and all the other essentials mentioned on the government websites that apply to your particular situation.

Why so much? If a major disaster occurs, it may take a few weeks for help to arrive. Even after a winter storm hits in a city in the United States, it frequently takes a week or more to restore electrical power to everyone. For example, in Lexington, Kentucky where I live, a February 2003 ice storm left about 2/3 of the city without electrical power, many for days, some for over a week, a few for a couple of weeks or longer.

Furthermore, in response to that 2003 Lexington winter storm, numerous utility-line repair people from states far away from Kentucky assisted, because their states were not affected. Also, the homes, stores, and other businesses in about 1/3 of Lexington were affected little. What if the outages had been more widespread?

If a major winter storm, earthquake, flood, or other disaster knocked out electrical power to much of the United States, there are not enough electrical line repair people to repair all those downed lines in a few days—or even a few weeks (or several weeks) in a very severe case. Depending on the type of disaster, roads may be damaged or flooded, trees may be down, hazardous chemicals may be released in the area, and all utilities (water, electricity, natural gas, phone service, etc.) may be cut off. Please prepare to shelter in your home for at least three weeks in case of an emergency. Board up windows if extremely high winds are expected.

If you haven't read the lists on the government websites mentioned earlier, I urge you to do so. Even if you've read a list before, do you remember it, and do you have it stocked? Most of the items on the lists are good for a wide variety of emergencies, not just relatively common ones like a winter storm, flood, hurricane, or earthquake.

Carbon Monoxide Detectors and Generators

Buy a battery-powered carbon monoxide detector. Several have died from carbon monoxide poisoning due to improper use of heating sources (generators, charcoal grills, kerosene heaters, gas heaters, etc.)

Remember, diesel-powered and gas-powered generators (as well as charcoal grills) must operate outside your residence. If you have a generator and fuel for it, please place it outside and ventilate it away from all dwellings. The American Red Cross website (http://www.redcross.org/prepare/disaster/power-outage/safe-generator-use)[27] is one of many sources providing more details on safely using generators.

Please don't underestimate the danger of generators. Here in Lexington, Kentucky radio station WVLK reported some years ago about one family that was smart enough to put their generator outside and vent it away from their home—but they vented it toward a neighbor's house. Fortunately, the neighbors felt ill effects and got medical attention. They lived. But a spokesperson for the Lexington Fire Department stated that the carbon monoxide level in the neighbor's home was several times the fatal limit, according to the WVLK news report.

Alternative Heating Source and Alternative Communication Methods

Try to have an alternative heating source that requires neither electricity nor natural gas, especially if you live in an isolated, rural area where a shelter is not available in case of a winter emergency. A wood stove, coal stove, oil stove, kerosene heater, fireplace, etc., can work.

Automobile exhaust is one major source of carbon monoxide, so please do not leave your car running in a garage or other enclosed area either.

Do seek to stay warm in cold weather though. If all else fails, putting everyone in one small room that is isolated from other areas and lighting a couple of oil lamps and candles will generate some heat. But, please be careful with fire. Provide at least a little ventilation to avoid either carbon monoxide poisoning or lack of oxygen due to the oil lamps and candles. And take steps to prevent a fire hazard. Standard safety procedures—but does anyone always follow all safety procedures? If we did, many accidents would be prevented. Bundle up in several layers of clothing to hold in warmth, too. Use blankets, sleeping bags, etc.

Try to plan in advance for some way to communicate with others without using a land-line phone, a cell phone, the Internet, a car, etc. Perhaps a satellite phone will be available nearby in an emergency center. An amateur radio operator may also be nearby. But even if such resources exist, you must be able to contact them. Downed power lines, felled trees, flooded streams, chemical fumes, and newly opened holes in the earth (in the case of an earthquake) may all impede your movement. The types of problems depend on the specific disaster.

Evacuation Plans

In addition, be prepared to evacuate your home if necessary. Keep the most essential items of your emergency supply kit handy in backpacks, the trunk of your car, or ready to put on your bicycle rack with short notice. Include appropriate clothing.

A three day supply (or less) of needed items may be all you can manage under these circumstances, especially if you must walk carrying the load.

If authorities urge you to evacuate due to imminent flooding or some other disaster, be ready and willing to do so when necessary. Keep your emergency kit packed and ready to go. If you wait, you may face enormous traffic jams and gas stations out of fuel—as New Orleans residents did with Hurricane Katrina in 2005.

Your evacuation plans need to consider various transportation methods. If airports, trains, and roads are so damaged (or overcrowded) that you can't use them to evacuate, you may need to carry your emergency kit a long distance on a bicycle rack while bicycling—or in a backpack while walking.

Be willing to bicycle or walk if necessary, as long as your physical condition allows it. If those who are physically fit leave on their own, it will free up emergency response personnel and equipment for the truly needy, such as the elderly and disabled living alone.

I own a bicycle with a metal rack on the back and a few backpacks. I keep two backpacks stocked with emergency supplies that I try to replace if necessary (due to food close to the expiration date, etc.) once or twice a year. I hope I never encounter a major disaster, but if I ever do these resources may be very useful.

Conclusion

I hope what I've written helps you prepare for an emergency if you face one. Please consider doing further research on this topic, too. For example, additional advance planning may be especially necessary for disasters like chemical spills and biological disasters that may require you to seal yourself in an airtight room for a period. Obviously, due to the limited air supply, this would hopefully only be for a few hours.

You can access lots of helpful emergency preparedness resources online, in bookstores, at the library, via phone, etc.,—if you plan in advance. In fact, the Ready.gov and FEMA websites I cited earlier in this chapter contain a wealth of additional disaster preparedness information besides the lists of suggested emergency kit contents.

If you haven't already done so, please take action now or soon to prepare for possible disasters. Please do plan ahead! And I think true Christians would help others plan ahead, too. Therefore, I urge you to help others prepare. Please urge others to take the steps advocated in this chapter, too.

Just as we need to decide what to do to prepare for a potential emergency situation, we also need to make many other decisions. For example, we decide whether or not to get any piercings or tattoos. In the next chapter, I discuss piercings and tattoos.

Chapter 35 Questions for Reflection and Discussion
1. Do you have an emergency kit? If so, is it completely stocked and do you periodically replace items to keep fresh ones in the kit?
2. Is a three week supply of items appropriate for your emergency kit or do you think it is too little or too much? Why?
3. Have you thought about how you would evacuate if necessary?

Chapter 36:
Piercings and Tattoos

Though adults may choose to get a part of their body pierced or tattooed, is that wise? Personally, I think not. I feel that Christians (and all people) do well if we take good care of ourselves. Putting unnecessary extra holes in body parts or injecting ink under the skin does not seem wise.

If you are considering getting a piercing or a tattoo, before doing so please consider the health risks and the effects on one's appearance. You can find numerous articles online that discuss these things.

Five Specific Reasons Not to Get a Tattoo or a Piercing

Below I discuss five specific reasons not to get a tattoo or a piercing:

- the risk of infection. Why risk a potentially life-threatening infection?
- the cost. Couldn't the money be better spent on something else?
- the effect on one's appearance. Many persons dislike seeing tattoos or piercings.
- the permanence. Removing tattoos is difficult, time consuming, and may not work well. Even the holes from piercings take time to heal, and the area may not return to its original appearance. Scarring can occur with tattoos and piercings.
- the pain. You can experience pain while getting a tattoo or piercing, as well as afterward.

Christian Tattoos and Concluding Thoughts

I know people who obtained tattoos of Jesus, of a cross, or of something else related to Christianity to demonstrate their faith. They frequently seem to sincerely feel that Christian tattoos help them in their Christian witness. But is it really necessary to acquire a tattoo to demonstrate one's faith? Do you think Jesus would want you to go to a tattoo parlor and get a tattoo or would he prefer for you to spend that money on food or other necessary items for the needy? I hope you agree with me that one's faith can be demonstrated better in other ways than by getting tattooed or pierced.

I realize persons sometimes have strong emotional reasons for getting tattoos or piercings. For example, they may desire to show love for a relative or friend. However, relationships change, as do ways of honoring and remembering those relationships. I feel that there are other ways to demonstrate one's love that don't disfigure one's body.

In conclusion, yes, adults of legal age have the option of getting tattoos or piercings. But I don't recommend getting one. And I certainly don't desire to get one myself.

Just as spending money on tattoos or piercings seems unnecessary, gambling seems to be a poor use of one's money. In the next chapter I discuss gambling.

Chapter 36 Questions for Reflection and Discussion
1. How do you feel about tattoos?
2. How do you feel about piercings?
3. Why do you think people who get piercings or tattoos do so?
4. Do you have any piercings or tattoos? If so, do you regret getting it/them?
5. Do you think pierced ears are more acceptable than piercings of the nose, tongue, navel, etc.? If so, why?

Chapter 37:
Gambling May Lead to Major Problems

Some view gambling as fun entertainment or an easy way to make money. I strongly disagree.

Even small friendly bets with friends can lead to disputes. For example, one person may be unwilling (or unable) to pay when they lose a bet. An argument may also occur over the exact terms of the bet. A friendship can be weakened or destroyed as the dispute over money escalates.

Many years ago I made some small, friendly bets with good friends. I also visited horse racing tracks here in Lexington, Kentucky at least twice, but I only placed one bet on one visit. And that wasn't really my money. I'll explain. I told a friend that I didn't intend to place any bets. But I did mention one horse that I thought had a good chance to win in one particular race—based on nothing scientific. He urged me to bet on it. When I refused, he gave me a small amount of money, $2 I think, to bet on the horse. I placed the bet but told him that if the horse won, the winnings were his. And before the race began, I insisted he take the ticket. I think I'd have been happy for him if the horse won, but it lost. This is the only time I've bet on a horse race.

Gambling too often leads to disagreements and lost money as I see it. I stopped making even small, friendly bets with friends, because I felt that disputes might erupt, as a few minor ones did.

Disputes can be even worse when the sums of money are large. And with organized gambling via slot machines, horse race tracks, lottery tickets, etc., there is "overhead," which is the term I use to refer to the amount of money the operator of the slot machines, race tracks, lottery, etc., keeps for various purposes rather than paying out to winners. In other words, people lose more than they win.

Even if all the money wagered was paid to the winners of bets, the only way someone could win at gambling would be for someone else to lose. That does not seem good to me. No useful product or service is produced by gambling that makes it worthwhile in my opinion. Furthermore, the minority of people who become compulsive gamblers cause significant problems for themselves—and in some cases problems for their families and friends, as well as others.

Some people likely gamble just for entertainment. And even persons buying losing lottery tickets may be happy in some way during the time between when they buy the ticket and the time they learn the results of the drawing—joyfully visualizing their potential winnings and how they can use them. Still, over the long term I feel these people would be happier not gambling in most cases. Furthermore, most of the people I know who buy lottery tickets here in Lexington, Kentucky are low income people who could likely better use the money for other things—including food, rent, utilities, and health care.

Sports Betting

Betting on sports adds up to a significant amount of money for many sports fans. Though I am not a big sports fan overall, I am a college basketball fanatic. It is one of my weaknesses.

Like millions of others, I fill out brackets online for the annual NCAA men's Division I college basketball tournament at some of the numerous websites that charge no entry fee for doing so. I feel that this uses time that could be spent more productively, and there is the risk that a group of people might seek to alter the outcome of games to increase their chances of winning a bracket. For example, someone could bribe players or coaches to not try to do their best. History records some cases of players taking such bribes to alter the outcome of games.

Many individuals pay money to enter workplace or school NCAA bracket contests. Many years ago, I entered a few such contests with friends at school. It was fun comparing picks and discussing the games, but it took some time away from studies, etc. This form of gambling likely hurts school and work productivity, in addition to costing everyone except the few winners money. At the end of the contests, I typically felt a bit down because of the money I'd spent on it, though it was a small amount. I feel that there are better ways to use one's time.

Perhaps completing one bracket just for the fun and not entering a contest would be a good alternative. But we in the United States seem to devote too much time and money to both gambling and sports.

Sports (as well as gambling) need to be kept in the proper perspective. College basketball is just one example of it, but I used college basketball as an example because following college basketball closely (especially University of Kentucky basketball) is one of my personal weaknesses. I do devote less time to it than I used to though, thanks to God.

Organized Gambling

Organized gambling seems to do much more harm than good. It seems especially sad that so many state governments are in the business of running lotteries, encouraging people to buy tickets. Many years ago, the state government in my home state of Kentucky initiated a state lottery to supposedly improve the state's finances. I feel that the state is in worse economic shape now than before the lottery—and likely has more compulsive gamblers, too. I think the lottery is partially responsible for this. In addition, I am ashamed of some of the advertisements run on television and radio to promote the state lottery.

Conclusion

I urge those who gamble with their money to please consider choosing alternative forms of entertainment and to find more ethical ways to try to make money than by gambling. Personally, I will try to devote less time to filling out the free NCAA tournament brackets in the future.

Just as I consider gambling a poor use of money, in most cases I feel buying neckties is a waste of money. In the next chapter I discuss buying and wearing neckties.

Chapter 37 Questions for Reflection and Discussion
1. How do you feel about gambling in general?
2. Do you think governments should conduct lotteries? If so, do you support stopping the often false or misleading advertising that promotes the lotteries?
3. What is your view toward casino gambling? How do you feel about betting on horse races?
4. Do you engage in "small, friendly bets" with friends? If so, have you ever had a dispute that threatened a friendship?
5. If you oppose gambling, do you believe filling out a bracket on a website for the NCAA men's Division I basketball tournament is wrong, even if no entry fee is charged?
6. How high do you think the potential is for players, coaches, officials, etc., to deliberately try to alter the outcome of a game to win a bet? How likely do you think it is that they would take a bribe from someone else to alter a game?

Chapter 38:
Neckties: Attractive? Elegant? Actually Unnecessary and Unsafe

It remains common for Christians to wear neckties to church (and to business functions, etc.). Why does a Christian man (or anyone) wear a necktie? Do neckties serve any useful purpose?

A colorful tie can be attractive, maybe even look elegant. However, wearing clothing just for appearance seems a waste, especially in an age when conservation and being environmentally friendly are emphasized. Ties seem pretentious and worldly—not what God or Christ would advocate.

Perhaps neckties originated from scarves worn in winter around the face to help protect people from cold and/or windy weather. Nicely tied, stylish scarves worn when weather conditions warranted them may have been the precursor of the necktie. But the ties commonly worn now, tied the way they are typically tied, serve no useful purpose that I comprehend.

Still, the wearing of neckties in public is a common practice in the United States and many other countries among persons in leadership positions in business, government, and religion. Certain formal parties and some restaurants also require a tie. In fact, so-called "black tie affairs" may require a black tie or more specifically a black bow tie, a tuxedo, and/or other formal apparel. Indeed, ties are traditional in some circles.

I think it is time to end the tradition of wearing ties.

Neckties cost money to purchase, take time to tie, may feel uncomfortable around one's neck, and are a potential safety hazard if they flap around loosely and get caught in machinery.

In contrast to ties, much of the clothing we wear serves a useful purpose. Shoes protect our feet. Undergarments, socks, pants, shirts, hats, and gloves provide us warmth, protect us from sunburn, and help guard our skin from injuries that might otherwise result as we contact various objects. But I submit that ties need to be either recycled into something more useful or discarded.

Personally, I have not worn a tie in several years and probably will not do so again unless I am in a situation where someone else requests it, such as for a job where wearing one is mandatory. Do you agree with me that wearing a tie is unnecessary, potentially unsafe, and a waste of time, as well as a waste of the money spent to buy it?

If we love and care for everyone regardless of circumstances, neither we nor they need to display a necktie as a status symbol or for any other reason that I can think of. In fact, try to avoid focusing on ties others wear.

Instead, focus your eyes on their faces, smile at them, and establish eye contact. Our actions, words, and our other apparel can suitably convey information about us to one another.

If you are required to wear a tie at work, please try to get the decision maker(s) for your workplace to read this two-page chapter and to change the policy requiring employees to wear ties. I think it would be great for everyone to avoid spending money buying ties and time tying them. Dedicate that money and time toward more productive and more enjoyable living. Will you do it?

Just as many men seem to wear ties unnecessarily, many women seem to wear high heel shoes unnecessarily. In the next chapter I discuss high heel shoes.

Chapter 38 Questions for Reflection and Discussion
1. How do you feel about wearing a tie?
2. If you wear one, will you stop wearing ties unless required to by an employer or someone else?
3. How much time and money do you think could be saved if persons stopped buying and wearing ties? Can you think of better ways to spend that time and money than on ties?

Chapter 39:
Wearing High Heel Shoes—Definite Health Risks—Any Benefit?

Women enjoy the right to wear shoes of their choice. But I wonder why so many choose to frequently wear high heel shoes (also called high-heeled shoes). A lot of women wear high-heeled shoes to church services (and other activities). Why does a Christian woman (or anyone) wear high heels?

I remember watching women struggle to walk in high-heeled shoes. I remember women talking about how their feet hurt at the end of the day after wearing high heels for several hours. Why do women punish themselves this way?

What is the purpose of a shoe? It seems to me that the main purposes of shoes are protecting one's feet and making it easier to walk and stand. Low-heeled shoes seem much better suited for this.

I think high-heeled shoes seem to be uncomfortable to wear, unsafe to walk in, and inappropriate to wear while driving a car. Furthermore, over the long term they can cause several problems for your feet—assuming you don't fall and suffer a severe accident in the short term wearing them.

I am not a medical professional and cannot give any medical advice. But if you like, you can research online and find numerous articles either written by medical professionals or that quote medical professionals, which report on the safety hazards of high-heeled shoes.

Can anyone cite any medical benefit to the average person from wearing high heels? Is there any reason for the average lady to wear high heels other than fashion? Is the desire to look fashionable the big appeal? If some fashion show (whether in Paris or in your hometown) portrays specific styles as being "in" this season, will women in your neighborhood rush in droves to buy the newly fashionable shoes? Please seek to resist the temptation.

I urge women to revolt peacefully against the persons/traditions/forces that lead them to purchase and wear high-heeled shoes. Instead, buy and wear comfortable walking shoes.

I am thankful men typically do not wear high heels. I personally have never worn them other than trying them on briefly. I hope the day will come soon when no employer finds high heels necessary for female employees. If your job requires them, you have my sympathy. I hope your employer reads this chapter and changes the requirement.

There are various theories on how high heels originated and why they became popular. You can find numerous articles online about the subject if it interests you. For my purposes here, I find it sufficient to state that I do not know of a logical reason (other than orders from an employer or someone else) for modern women to insert their feet into them at all. I certainly see no reason for ladies to wear them for hours daily while walking, working typical jobs, driving a car, or relaxing.

Indeed, I know of no good reason for buying or wearing high heel shoes unless an employer requires it (which seems discriminatory and is hopefully relatively rare). However, I am a man. Perhaps as a member of the male gender there is something I fail to understand on this topic.

Some women who wear high-heeled shoes at least sometimes and gave me feedback on their reason(s) for wearing them seemed to basically offer three reasons for wearing high heels: (1) to satisfy a job requirement, (2) to appear taller, and/or (3) to look more attractive. I sympathize with the job issue and hope employers will change that requirement, as I stated earlier. But I respectfully feel that the other two reasons do not justify undertaking the health risks of high heels.

If you know of a good reason for wearing high-heeled shoes, please write to tell me about it and why you think it is a good reason. Thanks!

One event that young ladies often wear high-heeled shoes to is a high school prom. In the next chapter I discuss high school proms.

Chapter 39 Questions for Reflection and Discussion
1. What do you think about wearing high-heeled shoes?
2. Do you see one or more good reasons for wearing them? If so, what?

Chapter 40:
Is the High School Prom Important? Maybe No

Should Christians attend their high school prom? If so, how should they behave when they attend?

Is prom night the most important evening of the year for a high school student? Or is the high school prom an unnecessary event that ought to be abolished? Or is the truth somewhere between the two?

A variety of attitudes exist toward high school proms. Many high school students devote a lot of time, money, and effort toward making prom night a special once in a lifetime event. Some rent limousines and tuxedos, buy special dresses, rent hotel rooms for after the prom, etc.

On the other hand, some students consider proms unimportant or even unnecessary—and do not even attend. Personally, I never attended my high school's prom and don't regret my decision—but I realize others were happy with their decisions to attend.

Let's first consider good reasons to consider skipping the prom, then look at ways teenagers who attend the prom can enjoy a fun, memorable experience with a reduced risk of suffering the major negative consequences many proms are notorious for.

Good Reasons Many (Including Me) Chose to Skip the Prom

Some of my closest friends and I were more focused on preparing for college and our other activities than the prom. For students who are busy preparing for college, active with hobbies, working at a fun (or necessary) job, heavily involved in a church group, busy with family events, or focused on enjoyable endeavors of some other type, the prom may not be very significant. Even some teenagers who considered their high school prom the most important event in their life at the time, valued it much less in hindsight—possibly even regretting what they did that night.

Students who consider high school a preparation for the beginning of adulthood may value getting ready for upcoming opportunities after high school graduation the most important thing during their secondary school years. The prom can be much less significant in this regard than the "in crowd" at a high school says. Believe me, there is life besides the prom!

It can be better to enjoy other fun activities in a way that requires less preparation time and money, as well as fewer risks, than a prom involves for a lot of teenagers. Why risk one's future and one's life for one event that consists of a few hours on one day?

I enjoyed my high school years without attending a prom. I do not regret choosing to skip high school proms. After high school I entered college at the University of Kentucky and found a wide variety of activities available there. College offered loads of opportunities to attend seminars, lectures, discussions, and a wide variety of sporting events, in addition to classes. Lots of tasty foods, new friends from various states and countries, and insights gained from various cultures made college a special experience. Numerous student organizations and volunteer opportunities exist on major college campuses like the University of Kentucky, too. I didn't mind that there was no college prom—and likely wouldn't have gone if there was one!

Even for high school graduates who forgo college, there are community clubs, careers, religious activities, etc., that can provide experiences that are more educational and rewarding in various ways—and less pretentious—than much of what a prom consists of.

Though I skipped the high school prom for secular reasons, many conservative religious groups oppose proms for reasons related to their faith. For example, some conservative Christians and conservative Muslims oppose proms. But, even within the Christian and Islamic faiths, a variety of individual views exist. For example, I know many Christians who attended their high school proms.

Alternatives to the Prom on Prom Night

By the way, if you choose to skip the prom, many other choices are available. Check your area to see if either a religious organization you respect or a trustworthy secular group offers some fun alternative event(s) on prom night. If not, perhaps you and some responsible teens (and parents) can plan something.

Sometimes events besides a prom can better lead to talking, laughing, and enjoying the company of friends in a relaxed, fun, secure atmosphere. Isn't that what many really want and need?

Getting together with friends in a safe, well-supervised place for board and card games, bowling, volleyball, other games, a tasty restaurant meal, and/or a huge variety of other activities can often be as much fun as the prom. Since these alternatives are typically much cheaper than the prom, they offer a further advantage by allowing teenagers to save money for college or some other future activity, while enjoying themselves in a safe place.

Personally, I think there are lots of cheaper alternative activities to participate in that are more fun and provide a better environment than the ostentatious and sometimes pretentious atmosphere of a prom—safer things, too. Far too many young people seem to risk their entire futures for the sake of one prom night.

In the above paragraphs I've mentioned some reasons to skip the prom that apply for many students. But, what seems ostentatious and pretentious to me may be appreciated by some others—who love the decorations, special apparel, luxury transportation, etc., that may accompany a prom and make it a "once in a lifetime" event.

If You Go: Enjoy a Very Special Prom Safely (and Keep the Prom in Perspective)

I realize prom night is a very special experience for a lot of teenagers. Even many years after graduating from high school a lot of people still talk about the fun that they had at the prom and share pictures that preserved a record of the event. A lot of individuals look back upon a high school prom as a highlight (or even the most memorable event) of their lives. For many of them, those prom tickets, the special dress or tuxedo, the limo, and hours spent decorating and making other preparations seem well worth it. And many prom attendees enjoyed a great night without the limo or expensive clothing—different approaches for different people.

One key to increasing the likelihood of a positive prom experience is to take precautions that reduce the risks. What can go wrong? Perhaps the biggest tragedy of prom night involves the reckless behavior so many high school students engage in. A drunk driving accident, an illegal drug slipped into a soft drink, or a casual sexual encounter on prom night can end a life in a second or negatively impact it forever through a severe injury, an unplanned pregnancy, and/or a sexually transmitted disease.

You may have read some of the numerous news reports about tragedies that have occurred on prom nights. These cause parents numerous worries. Teens need to be concerned also, as many are. Students, take steps to reduce the chance of something tragic happening to you. Yes, you! The Centers for Disease Control and Prevention (http://www.cdc.gov/family/prom/)[28] and FamilyEducation.com (http://life.familyeducation.com/teen/prom/36549.html)[29] are just two of the many sources that offer specific safety tips to help parents and teens enjoy a trouble-free prom night.

I encourage those who doubt the risks of premarital sex or drinking alcoholic beverages (or who desire more information on them) to read (or reread) chapter 27 in this book dealing with sexual abstinence until marriage and chapter 30 dealing with alcoholic beverages.

Please keep in mind also that, even if you attend the prom, you may desire to attend a structured, chaperoned event later in the evening after the prom is over to avoid the large number of problems that often occur at informal social events after the prom. If a quality event is not planned for after your high school's prom, consider initiating plans for one—with help from others.

If you choose to attend a prom, I hope you enjoy a fabulous time that you remember fondly afterward. Experience a delightful, safe, and memorable prom without endangering your life through casual sex, alcohol abuse, or other risky behaviors. Loads of fun can be enjoyed without taking major risks!

Concluding Comments

High school students must make up their own minds—often in consultation with parents, friends, and others—about whether or not to attend a prom. And in some cases parents may feel the need to make the decision for the student.

Please remember, no matter how the prom goes, it is only one day in one's life. And if you choose to miss it, rest assured that there are lots of wonderful future opportunities for fun and fellowship in a huge variety of activities.

Your future can contain even better and more memorable events, especially if you don't suffer due to risky behavior on prom night! Enjoy going—or not going—to your high school's prom!

This chapter and the earlier ones covered some things this author feels that authentic Christians believe and do. In the next chapter, I begin Part IV, which relates this real Christianity to some other things, beginning with atheism in the next chapter.

Chapter 40 Questions for Reflection and Discussion
1. How important do you think the high school prom is?

2. If you attended one, in hindsight do you feel it was overrated? Did you enjoy it? How does it rate among your experiences over the course of your lifetime?
3. Would you be willing to help develop and chaperone an alternative to the high school prom in your community?
4. Does your community have any structured events for after the prom? If so, what?

This chapter concludes Part III. Before going on to Part IV, please take time to review Part III. The questions below may help.
1. Do you agree that the specific behaviors advocated in this part are good ones for Christians to practice? Why or why not?
2. What specific behaviors would you add to the list? Which, if any, would you take off?
3. What steps could you take (and/or advocate for others to take) to behave more like a true Christian?

Part IV: Relationship Between Christianity and Some Other Things

Chapter 41:
Atheism and Atheist Madalyn Murray O'Hair

I entered the University of Kentucky in Lexington, Kentucky as an agnostic in 1976. I did not know whether or not God existed. I wanted to learn the truth, and I tried to be open-minded about various views, including those of atheism.

Religious groups on campus and the student chapter of an atheist organization sought to reach students with their messages. One of the persons who talked to me was the University of Kentucky student president of the campus atheist organization affiliated with famous atheist Madalyn Murray O'Hair. This student seemed to be a wonderful person with credibility.

Some time after this particular student spoke to me about atheism, I saw her again in the Student Center cafeteria. This was during the 1978-79 academic year. I walked up to her and, seeking the truth, politely asked her, "How do you know there is no God?" She replied nicely something like, "How do you know there is one?" I answered that I didn't and informed her that I was an agnostic.

She replied that she didn't have any way to prove there was no God, but she added that someone was coming to campus soon who could answer my question. She told me that Madalyn Murray O'Hair (probably the best known atheist in the country at the time) would be speaking on campus later in the semester and would have a question-and-answer session after her talk. This student encouraged me to attend and ask Ms. Murray O'Hair the same question I had asked her. She said Ms. O'Hair would be able to answer it. I was happy to hear this!

Madalyn Murray O'Hair's Speech and the Question-and-Answer Session Afterward

I looked forward with eager anticipation to Madalyn Murray O'Hair's speech. I was a shy person and doubted if I'd have the courage to speak up in public in front of an audience to ask the question. But I was confident that Ms. O'Hair would likely provide evidence to support atheism during her address. If not, perhaps someone else would ask a question similar to the one I wanted answered in the question-and-answer session afterward.

When Madalyn Murray O'Hair spoke in the University of Kentucky Student Center Ballroom in Lexington, Kentucky on Sunday, March 4, 1979, I was still an agnostic. But I was open-minded and seriously considering both atheism and Christianity. Perhaps I was also considering some other religions to some extent; however, atheism and Christianity interested me most, besides agnosticism.

I enjoyed attending seminars and lectures on various topics, but this one especially interested me. After hearing an impressive introduction of Madalyn Murray O'Hair, I listened attentively to her speech. I felt sure a person with so much formal education would present a clear, logical explanation for how she knew there was no God.

Her speech disappointed me. During her speech I didn't think she provided a convincing reason for being an atheist. She offered no conclusive proof that there was no God. I considered asking the question "How do you know there is no God?" myself during the Q&A session afterward. But, as I wrote earlier, I was a shy person. At the time I was a quiet, kind of introverted individual. Therefore, I was reluctant to walk up to a microphone placed in the audience and to speak up in public. However, I saw the line of people waiting to ask questions, and I hoped one of them would ask the question. And someone did!

I think the leader of the student atheist organization remembered me asking her that question, saw me there, and convinced one of her friends to ask the question of Ms. O'Hair when she saw I wasn't in line to ask the question. At least I think I saw her talking to the person who asked the question shortly before she asked it. So that's my guess.

At any rate, the questioner politely asked Ms. Murray O'Hair how she knew there was no God. I perked my ears expectantly, waiting for the famous atheist to deliver a well-thought-out answer. To my surprise, Ms. O'Hair responded in a loud and belligerent tone, "Well, how do you know there is one?" The questioner politely replied, "I don't. I'm an agnostic." At this, Ms. O'Hair softened her tone and more pleasantly credited the questioner for being "open-minded," and urged her to come up afterward to talk to her. Ms. O'Hair's belligerent initial response deeply disappointed me. I felt Ms. O'Hair had avoided the question by responding to it with a question due to her lack of a good answer. It was a technique I had observed others using on various occasions.

At the end of the Q&A session I sought to move toward the front to see if I could overhear Ms. O'Hair explaining/discussing with this questioner how she knew there was no God. It was a large crowd, and it took quite a while for me to work my way to the front from my position near the back. But I saw a person I recognized as being the leader of the University of Kentucky's student atheist chapter, whom I mentioned earlier, moving toward the front. She was just a little ways in front of me. The crowd parted to make room for her progression toward the front (after she announced her title as head of UK's student atheist chapter), and I followed close behind her.

After I got to the front I listened to Ms. O'Hair converse informally with people. I didn't hear a conversation about how she knew there was no God, nor did I recognize the person who had asked the question as being among those conversing with Ms. O'Hair. But I might not have recognized her, or she might have gotten to the front before me and spoken to Ms. O'Hair. I stood there at the front until the end of the informal discussion session when Madalyn Murray O'Hair prepared to leave.

Ms. O'Hair Thanks God

Thinking perhaps the questioner would address Ms. O'Hair as she exited, I moved straight across the room, which was now somewhat less crowded, and waited as Ms. O'Hair approached the area where I was, near the exit Ms. O'Hair was moving toward. As she approached me, she looked at me and seemed undecided, perhaps nervous. I read her lips or overheard as she expressed concerns to her security detail about me being there on the side of the auditorium—after her having seen me a few minutes earlier near the front. There were some uniformed officers with her (state, city, or university police, I guess, but I don't remember which), in addition to her own accompaniment detail, and likely she perceived peaceful me as a potential threat. She had received numerous threats from various persons over the years due to her beliefs (or lack of beliefs) and her activities in support of atheism.

Then she commented to those with her that she thought that I was her friend, and as she approached me she was going to drop her purse. She told them not to pick it up and that she thought no one else in the crowd would either, unless I did. She added that if I picked it up and handed it to her she was going to thank me. If I didn't pick it up, she was going to pick it up herself, quickly look at it as if to ensure everything was there, say "Thank God" loudly, then she and the security detail would quickly leave.

As she neared me, she did just that. She dropped her purse, picked it up, said "Thank God" loudly, then she and the security detail left quickly.

Effect on My Religious Beliefs

Largely as a result of that encounter and Ms. O'Hair avoiding the question about how she knew there was no God by responding to it belligerently with a question, I rejected atheism. I felt that if the most widely known proponent of atheism (Ms. O'Hair) apparently couldn't answer a direct question about knowing there was no God except by answering it with a question, how could anyone prove that there was no God?

I then became undecided between agnosticism and Christianity. I knew little about other religions besides Christianity. And I guess I considered them cults in a sense. At that time, I don't think I knew anyone who belonged to any religious faith other than Christianity, although I have met several followers of other faiths since then. (As a side note, over the years since hearing Ms. O'Hair, I have learned a little more about some major world religions other than Christianity. In chapter 43 I briefly discuss my perspective on some of them.)

Even as an agnostic I had said a prayer each evening since childhood and prayed at certain other times as well. I often felt I received answers to my prayers, but I didn't know if the answers came from my own inner thoughts, ESP from another person, God, some intelligent life form from another planet communicating in some way, or from some other source.

Several months after Ms. O'Hair's visit to campus I began prayerfully reading a Gideon New Testament with an open mind. Soon afterward I became a Christian. Earlier in this book, in Chapter 7 which is titled "How I Became a Christian—And How My Faith Has Evolved," I go into more detail on this.

My views have changed much over the years, and I am currently a very ecumenical Christian. For example, I don't believe in the Trinity—which is a subject I covered in chapter 8, titled "Jesus as Son of Man."

I respect followers of all faiths, as well as agnostics and atheists. But, although I respect atheists, I am confident that there is no way that any atheist can "prove" there is no God. Indeed, an unabridged dictionary probably contains a definition of a "god" that even an atheist would believe in.

It is perhaps ironic that Madalyn Murray O'Hair, the famous atheist, was at least partially directly responsible for my rejecting atheism. Perhaps I owe her a debt of gratitude for helping me progress toward becoming a Christian.

Now that I am a Christian, I consider prayer the most powerful force available to us as humans. I am guessing that Ms. O'Hair apparently never understood the power and positive influence of prayer. I feel blessed immeasurably by God and hope readers of this chapter (and book) are as well.

In addition to persons who claim that there is no God, there are many people who say they don't know whether or not God exists, agnostics. In the next chapter, I discuss agnosticism.

Chapter 41 Questions for Reflection and Discussion
1. What are your views about atheism?
2. If you are an atheist, what leads you to believe there is no God? Do you feel you can "prove" there is no God, or do you just accept on faith that there is no God?
3. Do you have close friends who are atheists? If so, have you ever asked them (nicely) how they know there is no God? If so, what was the response?

Chapter 42:
Agnosticism

I can empathize with agnostics, since for several years I was an agnostic myself. Since I discussed my own agnosticism briefly in Chapters 6, 7, and 41, I won't dwell on it here.

However, as one who used to be an agnostic, I have a great deal of respect for agnostics. I especially appreciate agnostics who thoughtfully study and consider various faiths with an open mind.

Obviously scientists cannot currently prove whether or not God exists. Atheists cannot prove God does not exist. Nor can believers prove that God exists. Belief comes from faith.

Agnostics wise enough to know that they cannot prove whether or not God exists and open-minded enough to seek and consider appropriate information from various religious faiths, as well as information from atheists and other agnostics, often come closer to attaining an unbiased perspective than any other group of people in my opinion.

However, some agnostics seem to become cynical, critical, and negative toward the views of others. Also, some agnostics seem unhappy, lacking the inner peace that believers frequently possess.

Personally, I know that I feel much more inner peace now that I'm a Christian. My times of prayer and meditation are much more enjoyable and rewarding than they were when I was an agnostic—though I was blessed with numerous productive periods of prayer and meditation even as an agnostic. As I mentioned in chapter 6, even when I was an agnostic I prayed regularly.

I firmly believe that agnostics who sincerely devote themselves regularly to prayer, meditation, or quietly thinking and planning in a relaxed atmosphere will benefit immensely from the insights gained during such periods of introspection. They may even become believers in a higher power in the sense of recognizing that an inaudible voice from some source often provides them wise counsel during such periods.

One reason I regard agnostics so highly is that they often seem to sincerely seek the truth—and recognize that they don't know the truth about whether or not God exists. Open-minded agnostics sincerely seeking the truth frequently come closer to finding it in the end than lifetime members of a particular Christian denomination do, in my humble opinion.

I urge agnostics to keep seeking the truth humbly with an open mind. Furthermore, I urge those who are not agnostics to be willing to answer questions from agnostics truthfully and compassionately. I am confident that agnostics who keep seeking the truth will in many (if not most) cases come to enjoy some type of faith in God, the highest righteous authority, a spiritual force greater than themselves or any human being.

In addition to atheists who don't believe in God and agnostics who don't know whether or not God exists, there are followers of various other religious faiths besides Christianity. In the next chapter I discuss religions other than Christianity.

Chapter 42 Questions for Reflection and Discussion
1. How do you feel about agnosticism?
2. If you are a Christian, what approach would you advocate using in witnessing to an agnostic?
3. If you are an agnostic, are you actively seeking the truth about whether or not God exists with an open mind? If not, why not?

Chapter 43:
Religions Other Than Christianity

All the world's religions offer some benefits to their adherents. And all major religions seem to share some basic truths.

For example, the golden rule (discussed in chapter 2) is a foundation of many of the world's major faiths in one form or another. A commandment to obey the highest righteous authority is common. And basic rules, laws, or commandments that advocate truthfulness, honesty, loving others, helping one another, etc., are common, too.

My knowledge of faiths other than Christianity is very limited. However, I do feel that the words credited to Buddha that translate into English as stating something like "be good and do good" provide excellent advice. This Buddhist teaching has some parallels in Jesus' teachings, as do many of the other basic tenets of Buddhism. Arguably, Buddhism is more like Christianity than either Judaism or Islam, which are the two major monotheistic religions besides Christianity.

Both Judaism and Islam have numerous rites or rituals that devout practitioners of the faith are to engage in. Buddhism, like Christianity, offers more freedom in its approach to worship. Some Buddhists are so ecumenical that they also consider themselves Shintoists, Hindus, Confucianists, Taoists, Muslims, Jews, or Christians. Indeed, Buddhism (and Confucianism) is in a sense based more on moral teachings than on faith in God.

Of course, followers of mainstream Christianity would deny the ability of a Christian to also be a Buddhist or a follower of another faith. Indeed, many (if not most) followers of each of the three main monotheistic religions (Judaism, Christianity, and Islam) seem to act as if their faith is the only true faith, their God the only true God. However, these three faiths share similar stories about certain patriarchs, such as Abraham and Moses.

Judaism offers a foundation for Christianity, and Jesus himself was a Jew. In fact, in a sense, early Christians could have been considered "reform Jews" rather than founders of a new religion. They apparently even used the Jewish scriptures before the New Testament was created.

Islam and Christianity also have several parallels. My reading of an English translation of the Qur'an (also spelled Quran, Koran, and Coran) in its entirety and my discussions with Muslim friends indicate that the radical Islamic fundamentalists who make the news headlines for their terrorist attacks are as far from true Islam as the radical fundamentalist Christians who bomb abortion clinics and advocate expelling all Muslims from the United States are from true Christianity.

But the "Holy wars" that are sometimes "legitimized" based on reading from certain passages in the Old Testament used by Jews and certain passages in the Qur'an used by Muslims contrast sharply to the teachings advocating love even for enemies that are in the New Testament. Also, the numerous Jewish commentaries and Islamic Hadiths impact the views of many Jews and Muslims, respectively. In contrast, true Christians focus much on the New Testament teachings of Jesus and Paul about loving others, a much smaller group of writings. Of course, in actual practice, many (most?) who claim to be Christians don't actually practice that love, and many Jews and Muslims interpret those Old Testament and Qur'an passages (and the related commentaries and Hadiths) differently than the ultraorthodox Jews and radical Islamists.

Numerous religions exist around the world besides those three monotheistic ones and Buddhism, the four I've focused on in this chapter. The others include Hinduism, Confucianism, Taoism, Shintoism, and various tribal religions. I feel that as a Christian it is not my duty to tell these followers of nonChristian faiths that they are going to hell for being heathens, but instead to learn from each of them, as I encounter these followers of various religions.

Thus, I can improve my own Christian faith and make it closer to the perfect faith God desires me to have. And by witnessing through a humble and honest Christian life, I obtain opportunities to be a positive influence on these followers of other faiths—and perhaps get the opportunity to convert one or more of them to Christianity, through the grace and guidance of God.

In fact, I urge Christians to read English translations of some of the teachings of Buddha and Confucius, as well as the Old Testament and much of the Qur'an. As I mentioned in chapter 1, I believe that followers of other faiths and even persons who follow no faith can be considered Christians in some cases. Jesus and Paul commanded us to love even our enemies, so I think we certainly need to love followers of other faiths, too. Who knows? Through our love, we may turn some unbelievers into believers.

I have visited an Islamic mosque and a Jewish synagogue and would love to visit other religious facilities of various religions. I think such interfaith visits can be informative and help bridge the gap between faiths.

As a Christian, I do believe that seeking to love one's enemies is one thing that puts followers of Christianity a step above the typical follower of most (if not all) other faiths. For example (as I stated earlier), both the Old Testament of Judaism and the English Translation of the Qur'an that I read advocate war against enemies under certain circumstances, in contrast to Jesus' and Paul's teachings in Christianity on loving enemies. Unfortunately, many Christians seem to share views on war that are closer to those of Judaism and Islam than to those espoused in the New Testament. If we Christians could and would consistently exhibit love for all, I am confident we would see such positive changes in the world that they would appear to be miraculous. Indeed, I think they would be miraculous in the sense that attaining them would take immense help from the higher power of God. Still, let's strive for this.

As a Christian, I believe that if one reads the New Testament prayerfully and interprets it properly, one can gain guidance from the highest righteous authority, God. However, I feel prayerfully reading some of the numerous Christian books besides the Bible that are available in Christian bookstores and libraries can lead to such insights from God, too. Maybe, through the Holy Spirit, God can grant you such insights from the words printed in this book. If so, God deserves the credit and not me.

Furthermore, at the risk of offending some New Testament Christians, I will state that prayerfully reading some of the writings of other faiths can be enlightening, too. Christians who read Buddha's Eightfold Path, Confucius's teachings on ethics, and certain passages in the Torah and Qur'an can find much wisdom—maybe even insights from God, the highest righteous authority.

I am confident God can and does use parts of these various texts to provide constructive guidance to human beings all around the world. As a Christian, I prefer the New Testament gospels to the other texts and devote more time to reading them than all the others put together. But each is beneficial in its own way.

Most Christians would do well to devote more time to reading the New Testament and the writings of other faiths prayerfully. Through this study, I think we will progress in our faith, in our commitment to God, and in our love for others, including followers of other faiths. Furthermore, by knowing more about other faiths, we can witness more effectively to their followers. And I confess my need to progress much further along in this study myself.

Let's seek to love one another, to pray for one another, and to treat one another with respect, regardless of beliefs or behavior. With God's help we can succeed at it.

In addition to knowing something about other religions, it is good for Christians to have a basic awareness of some other practices. In the next chapter I briefly discuss such things as witchcraft, kabbalah, freemasonry, astrology, and "magic," and urge readers to focus on obeying God.

Chapter 43 Questions for Reflection and Discussion
1. How do you feel about religions other than Christianity?
2. Do you believe it is possible for a person who does not claim to be a Christian to actively practice Christianity in a sense? Have your views on this issue changed as a result of your reading of this chapter and previous ones in the book?
3. What do you think separates Christianity from other religions?
4. Have you ever read an English translation of the Qur'an? Have you ever visited a mosque? Have you read the Old Testament in its entirety? Have you ever visited a Jewish synagogue? Have you read about Buddha's Eightfold Path? Have you attended a worship service of any other faith than Christianity (or whichever religion you practice personally)? If so, what was your impression?

Chapter 44: Witchcraft, Kabbalah, Freemasonry, Astrology, and "Magic"

Persons who get involved in subjects like witchcraft, kabbalah, Freemasonry, astrology, and "magic" run a risk of doing great harm to themselves and others. I personally am not involved in them.

Since I am not involved in them, I do not claim to be an expert on these phenomena. But I believe that one who prays and tests the spirits, then follows the Holy Spirit's righteous guidance may eventually be led into the "good" aspects of these secretive arts in some ways. I think following God or a godly mentor is the only appropriate approach, if one ever desires getting involved in such areas even in a very minor way.

When I referred to testing the spirits in the previous paragraph, I meant ensuring that the instructions one receives through the spirit are correct. God's Holy Spirit won't tell you to lie, steal, kill, injure someone, or do anything else that is unethical. Instead, the Holy Spirit will instruct one in the right path to take, good things to do.

To put it simply, I firmly believe that doing good things makes good things happen. This may be a virtually universal belief. At their best, witchcraft, kabbalah, Freemasonry, astrology, and "magic" probably can make good things happen—when controlled by God rather than by individual humans. But in this chapter I discuss some of the problems of each, when practiced by humans under a human authority.

Witchcraft

As a child, I did not even believe in witches or witchcraft. However, the Bible discusses them and instructs followers of God not to be involved in witchcraft (Deuteronomy 18:10; Galatians 5:20). The words of the Bible and various unusual/unexplained events lead me to believe in a form of witchcraft now. I discuss a few of these unusual/unexplained events in chapter 49, which I titled "Truth May Sometimes Seem Stranger Than Fiction."

Wicca is a recognized religion with a significant number of practitioners. At their best, practitioners of witchcraft presumably seek to do good things and thus make good things happen. The key is to do good works and provide blessings and love, not curses. But as a Christian, I prefer depending on prayer and Godly teachings. I feel that to the extent that witchcraft works, its practitioners do more harm than good unless they are controlled and led by God's Holy Spirit—if there is such a thing as a witch led by God.

Someday scientists and/or other wise individuals will likely discover the logical scientific principles behind such things as witchcraft and be able to control and use the principles for good. Unfortunately, currently even scientists sometimes misuse (or allow misuse of) their scientific advances for destructive purposes like nuclear weaponry, chemical warfare, etc.

Great power under human control tends to lead to corruption and destruction, unless the higher power of God's righteous authority is submitted to first and foremost. Please read that last sentence again—I consider it that important.

I am confident persons using witchcraft without the guidance of God (the highest righteous authority) or the wisdom to use their knowledge properly potentially do enormous harm. They may even alter the weather on a large scale for the worse. If you are laughing at the last sentence, please stop. I am serious. I feel that individual human spiritual powers concentrated together in great numbers and used selfishly and/or destructively can cause great damage and harm in multiple ways—to people, animals, property, and the planet.

By the way, many strange beliefs exist about witches. I remember vividly that when I was a boy in the mid 1960s, my sister on at least two occasions had a cat that died. My mom stated that she thought a neighbor was killing them because the neighbor thought my mom was a witch who changed into a cat and that by killing the cat she could stop the witchcraft. You may find that hard to believe, but it is the truth, if my memory is accurate. By the way, I never saw my mom change into a cat.

Kabbalah and Freemasonry (Even Religions) Are Similar to Witchcraft in Some Ways

I am uncertain where kabbalah (frequently spelled in various other ways such as kabala, kabbala, cabala, cabbala, cabbalah, or qabalah) originated and cannot provide a detailed description of it. Many claim it comes from Judaism, but numerous others believe it predates Judaism. Indeed, kabbalah seems related to numerous things, including Freemasonry, witchcraft, Judaism, and perhaps some other religions as well. Kabbalah may be a common element within several groups/organizations that use "secret arts" that are not shared with the public.

Many aspects of kabbalah may not be written anywhere, just passed down verbally to certain select individuals to keep them hidden from the public. My belief is that kabbalah (or its roots) goes back thousands of years, predating Judaism and Freemasonry, which adopted parts of it as their own. But I am writing as an outsider, rather than an insider.

As I stated regarding witchcraft, I think it is important to follow God, and the righteous guidance of the Holy Spirit after testing the spirits, rather than indulging in esoteric arts. Kabbalah and any powers inherent in it would be dangerous if abused.

Some rituals of witchcraft, Freemasonry, and certain religions (including some Jewish and Christian sects), seem to be secret, not shared publicly. For example, the Old Testament of the Bible mentions certain rituals (including sacrifices) that only priests could perform—and only in a certain way in a particular place. Even today, Jewish rabbis and other religious leaders probably are required to keep certain esoteric knowledge secret. Similarly, witchcraft and Freemasonry apparently require members to commit to secrecy regarding certain aspects of their practice. Many aspects are likely not known to the average practitioner of

Freemasonry or witchcraft, based on my limited reading about them in several publicly available sources. Certain secretive things within the groups may not even be recorded in any written records, as was mentioned earlier regarding kabbalah. And kabbalah may be the common denominator between witchcraft, Judaism, and Freemasonry. Or perhaps witchcraft predates kabbalah and serves as the origin of it.

The brotherhood, sisterhood, love, and commitment to help one another that are likely common within Freemasonry, Wicca, and kabbalah are good. But it is important that such brotherhood or sisterhood be subordinate to a commitment to obey God's righteous guidance. One must be willing and able to hold fellow followers accountable in a loving way, so that they obey God. Avoid using secrecy as a way to enable wrongdoing and cover up sins.

As Christianity teaches, sins need to be confessed, repented of, and a righteous life lived afterward, to the extent reasonably possible. I typically oppose secretive organizations due to the potential for abuses and prefer the openness of being truthful in a loving way toward all, even one's enemies, that Christianity advocates. In Chapter 3, titled "Be Truthful Always—Avoid Telling 'White Lies,' " I discussed being truthful in more detail.

Of course, some secrets might be better not spoken of or written about, as I also mentioned in Chapter 3. But I feel that practitioners of Freemasonry, Wicca, and kabbalah all may be committing serious abuses under the cloak of secrecy.

Astrology

Astrology is another field that I feel is dangerous to enter. Many (most?) of the horoscopes printed in newspapers and other mass media sources seem to be fiction, written just for entertainment. But some aspects of astrology may be genuine. It is logical that the positions of the planets and other heavenly bodies would impact events on Earth, as astronomers know they do. Gravitational pull is one reason. For example, tides on Earth are influenced by the moon. However, it also seems logical that humans on Earth can have little control over the immense variety of objects in the vastness of the universe.

For me, it is basically enough to know that a higher power created the vast universe and controls it. For those interested in reading a Christian perspective on the Zodiac, I recommend a book by the famous Presbyterian minister Dr. D. James Kennedy, titled *The Real Meaning of the Zodiac* (1989; Coral Ridge Ministries; compiled and edited by Nancy Britt from a sermon series by Dr. Kennedy on the Zodiac).

"Magic"

"Magic" often seems to be based on either calling up "spirits" or performing "miracles" through some special words/incantations. A mixing of certain substances to create a chemical/physical reaction is another approach to making "magic" happen. In the case of magicians, optical illusions and trickery are part of "magic," but I will ignore the cases of illusions and trickery for purposes of this discussion.

If enough is known about the principles behind it, "magic" is not really magic in my opinion. But many aspects of the secret arts likely have never been revealed publicly or become known to scientific researchers. Like other secret arts, I feel practicing "magic" is best avoided unless led by God. Hypnotism and ESP are sometimes considered a part of this "magic," and I discuss them in chapters 45 and 47, respectively.

Additional Thoughts on These Secretive Arts

As science advances, maybe things we now think of as either "magic" or "witchcraft" (or dismiss as not really happening) will be explained scientifically. For example, currently science indicates that human flight is impossible. But if a person is very slender with little weight in their chest/stomach and has very strong arms and very strong legs and develops the ability to move or "flap" both legs and both arms in the proper direction(s) fast enough, maybe someday a scientific study will indicate that such a person can fly. Such a view may not be any more ridiculous than the Wright Brothers' views when they began building their first aircraft. Who knows? Maybe there really are human witches who can fly—though I've never seen one of these flying witches.

I do believe that when a Christian or other person sincerely seeking to gain and apply God's righteous guidance prays, that the guidance received through what I call the "Holy Spirit" in some ways may involve the same powers that witches, kabbalists, freemasons, astrologers, and practitioners of "magic" use. But I think gaining and using such powers through unselfish prayer is far preferable to seeking to apply them personally and selfishly through "black magic" or one of the secret arts/organizations. Don't pray selfishly though.

Many books are available on the various occult arts. One very readable book that discusses several of these occult arts (and the dangers of becoming involved in them) is *Out from Darkness* (first printed, 1985; fifth edition, 1989) by Ben Alexander. His book states that he was a spiritualist medium before becoming a Christian.

I strongly urge readers to seek to find and obey God's righteous guidance rather than to seek powers through secretive arts for selfish or destructive purposes. As stated earlier, in chapter 49 I describe some unusual events, at least a few of which may be attributable to persons using these powers of the secretive arts. I firmly believe that abusing these powers can do much harm—in contrast to the good that following the Holy Spirit can lead to.

In a sense hypnotism is a secret art, a form of "magic." The next chapter discusses hypnotism.

Chapter 44 Questions for Reflection and Discussion
1. What are your views about witchcraft?
2. How do you feel about kabbalah?
3. Do you feel that there is a connection between Freemasonry and Christianity? Do you think there is a conflict when a Christian is also a Mason?

4. Do you believe in "magic"? If so, do you think its use is ethical?

Chapter 45:
Hypnotism

As a child, I wondered if hypnotism really worked or was just an illusion. My doubts were greatly reduced during my teenage years when someone apparently hypnotized several other people in my presence. Other incidents in later years eliminated my doubts.

Though I now know hypnotism works, I feel that it is generally better to avoid hypnotism. Let's live in the real world, rather than under a hypnotic spell. However, hypnotism is widely used by many for various purposes.

I want to make it clear that I have never studied hypnotism and don't know how to hypnotize people, nor do I desire to learn how to. But I have witnessed others being hypnotized on at least a few occasions since that day when I was a teenager and apparently have been hypnotized myself at least a few times.

I will briefly mention four additional cases of hypnotism among those that I know about besides that time when I was a teenager. (1) During a morning worship service at a church, one of the ministers apparently briefly hypnotized the entire congregation except for himself, the pastor, and me. (2) Once when I visited a different church, the minister apparently briefly hypnotized the entire congregation except for himself and me. Some ministers in a few Christian denominations apparently use hypnotism regularly in their worship services. (3) On another occasion, when I was in a meeting at a university, a few men there hypnotized some others in the meeting while the speaker told a personal story they apparently didn't want everyone to hear. (4) Once when I was walking to a store on a cold winter day wearing a ski mask, I decided to take a short cut. Normally I try to stay on sidewalks and avoid walking on others' private property. But it was very cold so I decided to take a short cut and walk through a bank drive-through lane. As I walked down the drive-through lane of the bank, I heard voices apparently coming from two women tellers inside the bank. One apparently said "hit him." The other replied, "I did, but he's still coming." Then the first one said something like, "hit him again, as hard as you can." The next thing I knew, I was walking in another direction perhaps a hundred feet away. One of the women apparently hypnotized me briefly, altered my direction, then released me from the hypnotic spell.

I know of at least a few other incidents of hypnotism, but to save space (and to avoid disclosing personal information about individuals that could be embarrassing) I'll omit mentioning them.

Some Purposes and Effects of Hypnotism

Apparently one main purpose of hypnotism is for use as a defensive weapon. For example, I guess someone could hypnotize a potential attacker to stop them, as a nonviolent form of self defense, as the bank tellers may have been doing to me, possibly thinking I might be a threat to them. But presumably it could be dangerous. If I had been forced to walk in front of a car while hypnotized, perhaps it could have been fatal. However, I do think that after I was released from the hypnotic spell by the bank teller(s) that I heard them discuss the possibility of my being hit by a car, and one of them said she was watching for cars as I was walking under the hypnotic spell.

Maybe Jesus used hypnotism as a defensive weapon in the situation described in Luke 4:28–30. But that is just speculation since scripture doesn't say. My opinion is that God has better powers than hypnotism for his true followers to use.

Hypnotism can also be used to alter behavior in other ways—for better or worse—by planting thoughts or instructions into a person's mind while they are under hypnosis. Also, memory apparently can be altered during hypnotism. Some memories apparently can be removed and false memories planted into the mind. And in cases where the hypnotized subjects are rendered physically immobile for a period of time, subjects apparently have no memory of events that occurred while they were hypnotized. Hypnotism alters persons' perceptions of reality.

Catholic priests, some other ministers, and others seem to use hypnotism as a tool to prevent one or more persons in church congregations (and/or other groups or individuals) from hearing something they are telling one or more other persons. I believe many store employees also use a form of hypnotism (or something similar to hypnotism) to refocus customers' eyes toward objects the customers want to purchase or that the employee(s) want the customer to purchase. Similarly, some women seem to deliberately refocus men's eyes as a way to flirt and to test a man's interest in them. I know personally there have been times that my eyes were refocused for some reason to areas I was not interested in looking at. I simply refocused my eyes in what I considered the proper direction, and I feel no harm was done.

In many cases, hypnotism is likely used constructively to help people. For example, some medical professionals use hypnotism as one tool to help persons with various problems. But I think hypnotism can potentially cause undesirable purchases in a store and inappropriate romantic relationships between persons, among other harmful effects. Even medical professionals probably misuse hypnotism (deliberately or inadvertently) in at least some cases. For example, there are apparently cases of false memories being planted in people while they were under hypnosis by a medical professional.

I am not a medical professional, so I can't give any medical advice. However, I believe that there are better ways of handling most (if not all) situations than by resorting to hypnotism. I feel hypnotism can be very dangerous if abused and is unnecessary in most, if not all, cases. But I confess that my knowledge about it is very limited compared to that of those who have studied it extensively and practice it professionally. As I stated earlier, I do not know how to hypnotize people and don't desire to learn.

I hope this chapter succeeded in alerting readers to the facts that hypnotism works and that it can be dangerous if used by amateurs or abused by well-trained professionals. If any of you are hypnotists, please use hypnotism responsibly or not at all.

Finally, I think hypnotism may play a role in some mental illnesses. For example, if a hypnotist creates false memories for someone while they are under hypnosis, it distorts their view of reality. In the next chapter I discuss mental illness.

Chapter 45 Questions for Reflection and Discussion
1. If you know you have been hypnotized in the past, how do you feel about being hypnotized?
2. How do you feel about some ministers using hypnotism regularly on members of their congregations?
3. Have you ever practiced hypnotism? If so, what is your opinion about practicing hypnotism?
4. Do you think hypnotism should be regulated or prohibited? If so, how do you propose accomplishing its regulation or prohibition?

Chapter 46:
Mental Illness (Bipolar Disorder, etc.)

I think there is often very little difference between mental illness (or even insanity) and genius. Many geniuses would likely have been considered insane if their ideas hadn't worked out. Perhaps many "insane" people tried to fly before the "genius" Wright brothers succeeded in doing so.

Persons who exhibit a different view of reality than the normal one may be insane or they may be specially gifted. Jesus certainly elicited a variety of reactions from different people, including some who thought he was "beside himself" on at least one occasion as part of Mark 3:21 (KJV) puts it. To some extent, society's view of whether a person is "insane" or a "genius" depends on whether future events eventually prove their ideas to be ridiculous or a major advance.

Several years ago, a series of unusual events/coincidences and my way of speaking about them led to a series of things that resulted in a few brief psychiatric hospitalizations and outpatient psychiatric treatment for me in 1993–1996. God willing, I may elaborate more on that at some future time, if I feel it is the right thing to do.

In some ways, that period was a difficult time, and I certainly regret some of the things I said and did during that time, but I prefer not to focus upon it. I was blessed immeasurably during that time, and I am blessed immeasurably now, just as I always have been. And though I took lithium for a period of time during that 1993 to 1996 period for a diagnosis of a mild case of bipolar disorder, I have not taken any since 1996. I only take a daily multivitamin now.

Fortunately, my psychiatric illness was minor compared to the psychiatric illnesses of many others. In fact, maybe we are all mentally ill to some extent in one way or another, and if/when one or more traumatic events occur, whatever underlying condition(s) we have become worse.

However, as we seek to do the right thing, to submit our thoughts to God's perfect control, I think the Lord enables us to deal with issues appropriately. Chemical imbalances in the body may be the root of some mental disorders. But I think tender loving care helps correct many problems—and may even correct such chemical imbalances in some cases if they occur. But I am not a medical professional and cannot give any medical advice.

In the past the United States government (and others) conducted mind-control experiments. Sometimes the experiments involved mind-altering drugs like LSD. And these experiments likely contributed to at least some mental disorders suffered by various persons. Fortunately, I was never subjected to any mind-altering drugs by the government—at least as far as I know.

You can read more in numerous sources about the United States government "Project MKULTRA" mind-control experiments that sometimes involved the use of LSD on unsuspecting people. Three of these sources are the three pieces linked to at the end of this sentence, on the websites of the *New York Times* (https://www.nytimes.com/packages/pdf/national/13inmate_ProjectMKULTRA.pdf),[30] the *Los Angeles Times* (http://articles.latimes.com/1999/apr/04/local/me-24126),[31] and *Time* (http://content.time.com/time/specials/packages/article/0,28804,2008962_2008964_2008992,00.html).[32] I don't know if I was ever a part of a government experiment or not.

At any rate, I likely received some benefits from my hospitalizations and psychiatric outpatient treatment (and perhaps even from the lithium) during certain periods during 1993 to 1996. But just the geographic change of relocating to a different town/city (I didn't live in a town with a psychiatric hospital during that time period.) and the fellowship with others (patients and staff) did much good in my opinion—probably much more good than the lithium or the other psychiatric treatment provided by the medical professionals, as I see it.

I began taking a lower dosage of lithium than was prescribed without any problems. When my prescription came due for renewal, an enlightened psychiatrist formally reduced my prescribed dosage by 50%. And I haven't taken lithium at all since 1996.

As I see it, a daily morning walk, a new more suitable geographical location, quality loving friends and family, etc., in many cases can do more good than a hospital stay or a prescribed drug. The grace of God, friends, family, exercise, diet, and probably to some extent living in a larger and more diverse city have apparently cured my mild psychiatric ailment, as I see it. But I repeat that I am not a medical professional, so I can't give any medical advice.

Perhaps in a sense the artificial highs and lows created in certain worship services, as well as by illegal drug use, etc., have similarities to the highs and lows of persons diagnosed with bipolar disorder—and some of the negative effects may be similar, too. In the case of illegal drug use, additional life-threatening negative effects may also occur, as well as legal problems.

And a person being extremely careful to double-check or triple-check something shares some similarities with those suffering from obsessive-compulsive disorder. And a person who thinks he or she hears the inaudible voice of God during a worship service or while praying at home is somewhat similar to a paranoid-schizophrenic hearing voices.

Indeed, when a psychiatric disorder is relatively minor and used responsibly in a way that is beneficial, it may be a blessing. Maybe many geniuses are gifted to hear voices guiding them truthfully to help them develop their ideas. Triple-checking prevents accidents, so obsessive-compulsive disorder in moderation can perhaps be beneficial. And those artificial highs of certain people with bipolar disorder may lead to great creations in at least a few cases.

But persons ought not listen to and obey "false voices" that give them instructions to do wrong. And checking something ten times (or more) would at least seem to be a time consuming obsessive-compulsive trait. If you've already checked something three times and feel led to check it again, perhaps it's time to tell that inner voice that you've already triple-checked the item, and you are going to ignore the false spirit (or as it could perhaps be called, "witch's voice"), and link to God and move on to the next thing on God's agenda for you.

Also, when a person's mood swings are excessive and detrimental, it is certainly a problem. In my case, even the psychiatrists who diagnosed me seemed to think I only had a mild psychiatric disorder. In fact, I think at least one of them thought I was normal. Perhaps I was just temporarily stressed out by certain extremely stressful events.

As I stated earlier, I am not a medical professional and can't give any medical advice. But I do think we in the United States are too prone to take medicines for things that can often be treated better in other ways by improving the quality of our: diet, exercise, work, recreational activities, personal relationships, geographical locations, etc. Reducing stress by avoiding certain stressful situations and stressful relationships is helpful, too. Even normal people behave abnormally when subjected to extremely stressful situations.

Just moving to a new area with a better job market or a better climate may help some people. But be careful about moving away from one's support group.

Taking corrective actions early could do much to prevent a lot of the tragic endings that occur in the cases of numerous individuals diagnosed with mental illnesses. I believe that much mental illness (especially a large percentage of the severe cases) originates from some form of physical, mental, spiritual, or emotional abuse suffered at some point in a person's life.

Just following the simple teaching credited to Buddha of "be good and do good" and Jesus' teaching to love even one's enemies could do much to make individuals and the world better, if we practiced these two teachings all the time. If we all seek to help one another, we can do much to treat and cure a lot of problems, as I see it. Let's all seek to help one another when reasonably possible. I am grateful to all those who helped me.

In some cases I think persons perceived as being mentally ill actually are blessed with a form of ESP. In the next chapter I discuss ESP.

Chapter 46 Questions for Reflection and Discussion
1. What is your opinion about the view that in some cases there is little distinction between one who is mentally ill and one who is a genius?
2. Have you experienced mental illness? If so, do you feel comfortable talking about your experience with it?
3. How do you feel about mind control experiments conducted by the United States government and others?
4. How do you feel about current medical treatment methods for psychiatric disorders? Do you think future advances will lead to major changes in the treatment of mental illnesses?

Chapter 47:
ESP (Extrasensory Perception)

I am a firm believer that extrasensory perception (ESP) exists. Some of my own experiences that I discuss in Chapter 49 involved a form of ESP in my opinion. Scientific studies even support ESP's existence to some extent. You can research online to find links to some of these studies if you like.

My guess is that even the most knowledgeable scientists understand only a little about how the human mind functions. I believe we have abilities, including untapped abilities, that are virtually unbelievable. These include ESP.

Part of the way ESP functions involves an ability of at least some humans to communicate with at least some other humans who are too far away to communicate with by normal speech or eye contact. I don't know how this works, but perhaps the human mind somehow functions similar to a wireless phone system. In chapter 49 I briefly discuss a few of the personal experiences I have had regarding this.

One individual can even transmit thoughts into a second individual's dreams while the second individual is sleeping, thus altering those dreams. Decades ago, a journal article titled "An Experimental Approach to Dreams and Telepathy: II. Report of Three Studies" in the March 1970 issue of the *American Journal of Psychiatry* discussed a scientific study by Montague Ullman, M.D., and Stanley Krippner, Ph.D., regarding this topic. I first read about the study on page 254 of M. Scott Peck's 1978 book, *The Road Less Traveled* (published by the Touchstone imprint of Simon & Schuster), then went to the University of Kentucky Medical Library and found the actual journal article. The article amazed me. I encourage you to consider reading at least part of it.

I feel that on at least a few occasions others have transmitted thoughts to me to alter my dreams, but a scientific study hasn't been done on me, so you'll just have to accept (or not accept) my opinion. I may elaborate more on this topic in future writings, if I feel it will be beneficial to do so. I will end this brief discussion about dreams by stating that I feel strongly that it is important that no one ever alter anyone's dreams in an effort to do harm.

I firmly believe that ESP is a gift from our Creator to enable us to cope better during our lives on Earth. Therefore, it is important to use this gift wisely to help ourselves and others. It is important not to abuse it or dismiss it as unimportant.

It is also important to seek to separate true ESP from fakery. I feel that many individuals fake ESP for their own selfish purposes. But the fact that numerous fakes exist does not mean that real ESP doesn't exist.

In my own life I have experienced several unusual situations that I attribute to a form of ESP. God willing, I hope to elaborate more on some of them at a future time (in addition to the few discussed briefly in chapter 49).

Some believe that certain forms of ESP are communication to humans from advanced life forms beyond Earth. In the next chapter I discuss extraterrestrial life.

Chapter 47 Questions for Reflection and Discussion
1. Have you ever experienced something that you attribute to ESP? If so, what?
2. Do you agree that ESP is a gift from our Creator to help us?
3. Are you one of those who don't believe in ESP? If so, what might alter your disbelief?

Chapter 48:
Extraterrestrial Life

Given the vast size of the universe, it seems statistically likely that there is life out there somewhere. A huge number of stars and planets exist; our astronomers have no reasonable idea how many. Scientists don't know the size of the universe—or if it is the only universe. It would be far more unbelievable if out of all the planets in the universe only Earth contains life than if there are several other planets with life of some type. Some type of life may even exist on stars or somewhere else besides on planets.

In my humble opinion, there is intelligent life out there somewhere that is so far advanced beyond us that for lack of a better word we might call it "God" or "angels." Such life could exhibit powers we can't imagine and could observe us in ways we can't think of.

Perhaps even now this extraterrestrial life watches us. It may even protect us in some ways, preventing us from going too far overboard in our wars, just as we sometimes care for nonhuman creatures on Earth. I like to think that such intelligent life would help care for lower life forms—perhaps in ways lower life forms couldn't recognize or detect.

But just as we humans don't always show a lot of concern about injuring ants as we walk along sidewalks and often don't think about hurting worms when digging holes, such intelligent life forms may not show enormous concern for us when their minds and actions are focused on issues they consider more important to them.

Numerous persons have speculated that alien life visited the Earth in our past. Perhaps the best known of these is Erich Von Daniken, who wrote a best-selling book discussing this topic in detail. His book got the title *Chariots of the Gods?* when translated into English, and Von Daniken followed that book with some others on the same subject. Another popular book on this topic is *The Spaceships of Ezekiel* by Josef F. Blumrich.

I believe that intelligent life does exist elsewhere and that this life is likely to find us before we find it. Maybe it already has. And maybe it is helping us develop into better citizens of the universe—helping us in ways we don't yet comprehend.

However, given my very limited knowledge and wisdom, I prefer to trust in God to deal with issues like intelligent life from another planet unless or until such life is proven to exist—and perhaps even then. Maybe even my prayers to God are reaching intelligent alien life forms that serve as God's instruments to comprehend and answer prayers. At any rate, thank you to whichever higher righteous authority answers my prayers. And, as a Christian, I do call the highest righteous authority God.

The concept of life existing beyond Earth may seem unbelievable (or almost unbelievable) to many. However, numerous true occurrences seem almost unbelievable. In the next chapter I discuss some very unusual events that really happened—if my memory is correct.

Chapter 48 Questions for Reflection and Discussion
1. How likely do you think it is that life exists elsewhere in the universe? Why do you feel as you do?
2. Do you think it is possible that some type of intelligent life from another planet (or elsewhere in the universe) is watching us now?
3. Do you think our ancestors may have referred to alien life as "angels" and "God" for lack of better terms? How do you see the relationship between God and any other life forms in the universe?
4. Even if intelligent life exists elsewhere that is far superior to human life on Earth, do you feel that a higher power, God, is the creator of both that life and us?

Chapter 49:
Truth May Sometimes Seem Stranger Than Fiction

Often true stories are so extraordinary that those who didn't experience or observe them firsthand find them unbelievable. Several incidents I have personally experienced in my own life or learned about from others seem unbelievable. A few of them seem almost as "miraculous" as some of the "miracles" described in the Bible—and not always in a positive way. Perhaps God endows us with enormous powers of hearing, seeing, thinking, etc., that we seldom develop or use as God desires.

Though the events described in this chapter may not relate directly to Christianity, I feel their unusual nature offers support for the "miracles" described in the Bible, and I wanted to include them. To help protect others from undesired publicity, etc., in most cases described in this chapter I have omitted names and personal descriptions of other individuals involved. I realize this may make it hard for readers to find independent verification for the incidents, but I feel it is necessary. I decided not to include a few perhaps even more unbelievable incidents due to the inability to sufficiently make the identities of others involved anonymous while accurately detailing the stories.

I realize many readers will find even the incidents I included unbelievable. That is one reason I have placed them in one chapter near the end of the book. Still, I feel it is important to include them.

Though I number them for convenience, they are not necessarily in any particular order. Below I discuss a few very unusual events that really happened—if my memory is correct.

(1) Brief Sharp Eye Pain

During a visit to Washington, D.C., several years ago, as I rode an escalator up from the subway to street level, several persons in a hurry were walking quickly up past me while I stood stationary on the moving escalator. I thought they were being rude, and looked them in the eye indicating it. Someone below me said something like "he better watch it, or someone will hit him." I kept doing it, then suddenly when I looked at one person, I felt a brief sharp eye pain. I got the impression that the eye pain was to cue me that people considered it rude to look at people as I was doing rather than standing on the right side of the escalator step to politely let people pass me on the left.

After this, as I looked down at the bottom of the escalator, I noticed that there were several people lining up to get on, so it seemed to be rush hour. However, I would have preferred someone simply tell me it was rush hour and a long line was developing at the bottom of the escalator, so please move to the right to let people pass—rather than give me the brief eye pain. I could have even walked up the escalator myself instead of riding passively had I known. I probably should have been more observant.

I also felt that brief sharp eye pain on at least one other occasion, also several years ago, here in Kentucky. I discussed that incident briefly earlier, in chapter 15, titled " 'Miraculous' Healings and 'Speaking in Tongues.' " Is there a logical reason for this eye pain? Is causing it a power certain people have? Maybe I should pray about what to do as soon as I hear a voice saying something about "hit him."

(2) Brief Chest Pains

On several occasions in the 1990s (and on a few occasions since), I experienced a brief sharp chest pain. I got the impression that the pain was caused by certain persons looking at me and focusing their eyes and/or thoughts on me in some particular way to deliberately cause it. Below I describe one specific instance.

Once I experienced the brief chest pain during a visit to New York City. I was walking on the Brooklyn Heights Promenade and saw some benches. I noticed that they were all empty and sat down on one to enjoy the view. After a few minutes, I thought I ought to get up so others could sit down; surprisingly, I saw that the other benches were all still empty, despite the large number of people in the area. I wondered why. I saw no sign saying people could not sit on the benches, nor did I see a sign limiting how long one could sit on them. Still, I felt that somehow they were deliberately kept empty. I prayed about how the benches were kept empty. Then I felt a brief sharp pain in my chest, and an inaudible voice stated "that's how we do it." I can understand the need to have a method of keeping persons from monopolizing the benches, but I hope there is a better way to do it than causing a brief sharp chest pain.

My guess is that some people apparently have the power to cause others to experience chest pains, perhaps as a way to control their behavior. I wonder if this could be the cause of some heart attacks?

The few people I mentioned the brief chest pains to stated that they were my imagination. However, the pains certainly felt real, though they only lasted a second or a fraction of a second each. Thankfully, I haven't felt any recently, but what caused these brief pains? What can or should be done to prevent me or anyone from experiencing them? If they are a method of controlling behavior, I like to think that there is a better one.

(3) My Paternal Grandmother's Funeral: Did She Move Her Eyes?

I remember attending my paternal grandmother's funeral in Floyd County, Kentucky, when I was five years old. It is one of my earliest memories. Perhaps one reason I remember it so well is that on the drive to it mom repeatedly told me how important it was for me to behave, stating that my grandmother would be up front in a casket, but I couldn't go up to her. Another reason I remember it so well is something very unusual that happened there.

When we got to the funeral, actually the casket was in the back of the room, and so I asked mom if I could walk over and look at it. I think she asked dad if it was okay and he agreed it was. So I did. As I looked at my grandmother in the casket, I saw her eyes "sparkle" and move a few times. I told mom at least a few times that I thought my grandmother was alive.

I even thought I heard my grandmother ask me to climb up into the casket. I thought I heard her say that at least a couple more times, so I started to do so. I thought obeying her voice might revive her and make her happy. Then mom came over and got me before I could climb up. As I turned around, I saw the man up front had stopped speaking and several people had turned around to look at the back where we were (I think we had arrived late and though my aunt, dad's sister, came back to say she'd saved seats up front for us, dad said we'd stay in the back). I asked if the service was over, and I think mom said no. I asked why the man had stopped talking and people were turned around in their seats looking back, and mom said I had created a scene that interrupted. I guess I did.

On at least a few occasions there at the funeral I had thought I saw my grandmother's eyes move, thought she was alive, and even thought she was talking to me. After I told mom about the eyes moving and begged her to look, she walked over to look to appease me. Mom was looking once as my grandmother's eyes moved. After that, I heard mom tell dad that she thought she saw his mom's eyes move, too; she asked him to look, but he didn't. He thought it was crazy, and even at age five I could understand why. By the way, mom didn't remember this incident when I described it to her many years later. Was I a five-year-old having an illusion? Is my memory faulty?

(4) Postal Service Conversation Overheard About Oklahoma

During part of the mid1980s I worked for the U.S. Postal Service in Lexington, Kentucky, at the Nandino Boulevard mail sorting facility. We workers typically dressed in casual clothes since we worked in the back where we were typically out of public sight. Though we wore casual clothes, on a few nights several persons in dress clothes wearing ties showed up and began walking laps around the mail sorting facility.

I asked some other workers who these strangers were and why they were there, but the workers I asked didn't seem to know. Then one night as this group of well-dressed persons walked past the area where I worked, another worker asked one of them something like, "When are those people supposed to be killed at that Post Office in Oklahoma?" The other person replied something like, "How do you know about that? Nobody is supposed to know about it. If people know about it, it won't happen." After a very brief hesitation, he added, "Maybe it shouldn't happen."

The worker and the other person also exchanged a few other comments. I don't remember their exact words and may not have heard them all originally. But among the comments, I think the other person said something about the worker picking me to overhear the conversation. I got the impression that they had planned in advance to have a conversation on this subject and at least one of them wanted another person to overhear. The person who had been walking laps with the group said something like "I don't trust all these persons I'm walking with, though I do most of them, and they were carefully selected for this." This indicated to me that the persons chosen to walk laps around the facility were carefully selected.

Was this a joke? Did someone tell my coworker to ask that question about persons being killed at a Post Office in Oklahoma? I don't know. He asked the question loudly enough that at least a few of the other persons in dress clothes presumably heard it in addition to the one who answered him. A specific date or a specific location in Oklahoma wasn't mentioned, but I don't think it was very many days after that when several persons were killed at a U.S. Postal Service facility in Edmond, Oklahoma, apparently by a crazed individual.

I wonder if this was a planned thing or a coincidence. Could it have been some type of government mind control experiment? Did someone tell my coworker to ask that question?

Why were those persons in dress clothes all walking laps around the building? Did my thinking about it somehow make what happened in Oklahoma happen? I was scared after the tragedy in Oklahoma occurred and wanted to talk to my coworker to ask him about the question he asked, but he was absent for quite a while afterward and the coworkers I asked said they didn't know where he was at. I thought I heard one of them whisper to another person about hearing that he was psychiatrically hospitalized, but I'm not sure.

No one ever spoke to me about the specific details of that conversation again, and I was apparently followed around by several people for at least a few years afterward and received what I interpreted as a few veiled death threats. On at least a couple of occasions, when I tried to approach one of those following me, he retreated.

Out of fear, I didn't speak to anyone or write anyone about the incident until years later. The few people I've spoken to about the incident seemed to not take it seriously or to have been scared. One specifically told me to never speak about it again, and said he had orders to kill me if I did.

For some reason, I did not ask the coworker who asked that question about Oklahoma why he asked it, when he did return to work. For one thing, I think we typically worked in different areas then. Also, due to my being a temporary worker at the time I heard the conversation, I wasn't there long afterward myself, though I was called back to work later. When I finally did happen to see him there, as he walked up to me, he instructed me not to "say anything about the thing we both know because we are being watched" or words similar to that. I interpreted this to mean that as we talked we were being watched to see what we spoke about, since this was the first time the two of us had been together since the Oklahoma shootings.

Years later, long after I had left my work for the Postal Service, when I finally phoned my former coworker who had asked the question and described to him my memory of the conversation, he said he didn't remember it. One possible reason for his apparent memory lapse is the fact that when I spoke to him on the phone, speaking extemporaneously, my description of the conversation I had overheard about Oklahoma was not completely accurate, due to my inadvertently misspeaking. Another possibility is fear; he may have gotten threats as I did. I know I had plenty of fear after the Oklahoma shootings, due to what I perceived as veiled threats, due to the people following me around that didn't speak to me and retreated from me when I approached them, and due to some other unusual occurrences soon afterward. If all those people in the dress clothes circling around our postal facility work area knew what happened, I wondered why nothing was reported in the media about it.

I waited years to write about this. Initially my hesitation was due to fear, then later when I prayed about it, I felt that the time was not yet right to write about it—until recent years. I would love to elaborate a bit more on what I went through during the period after the Oklahoma shootings as a result of them and the conversation I overheard, but I feel that it would do more harm than good at this time.

It is possible that my memory is faulty, but I believe that this account written here is accurate. Memories can be faulty, however, and the conversation I remember overhearing (as well as the tragedy in Oklahoma) took place over 30 years ago (in 1986).

(5) Witch's Fire?

Several years ago, on an occasion when I was doing volunteer work helping another person at a location in Kentucky I won't disclose, the other individual became frustrated and upset about something. Perhaps he felt that I wasn't helping enough. And I wasn't doing much; I was inexperienced at the particular task and unsure what to do.

Suddenly I saw what looked like a stream of fire in front of me. It looked like images I've seen on fictional television shows of fire coming from the mouths of fire-breathing dragons. Another person who was there said that the other person had made "witch's fire" come out of my eyes.

I don't know where the "fire" came from, but it did seem to be directly in front of me. It disappeared very quickly, perhaps as quickly as it appeared, and it apparently caused no damage. At least two of us saw it—or saw something. What was it? Could it have been an optical illusion?

(6) Eyes Heating a Wedding Ring to Burn a Finger?

At a time I won't disclose and at a location in Kentucky I won't disclose, I was working with a particular person. On one occasion, our hands accidentally touched as we worked, and I tried focusing my eyes on her wedding ring to reduce the attraction I felt toward her. However, my vision seemed a bit blurred for a brief period, so I couldn't. Then suddenly my eyes focused directly on her ring instantly, like they had been directed there by an outside power. I got the impression that she used some spiritual power to somehow help my eyes focus. But I don't know.

At any rate, I saw a flash of light and her wedding ring glowed like bright sunlight was reflecting off it. I blinked, then looked again to verify that it wasn't an illusion. The wedding ring still glowed. I was going to draw her attention to the unusual appearance of her ring, but before I could, she ran off to rinse her finger and told someone that her finger was burned. Apparently somehow my eyes had focused on her ring in a way that caused the ring to get hot enough to burn her finger. I felt terrible about it. What caused that?

(7) Hearing Conversations Far Away or Reading Others' Unspoken Thoughts

On several occasions, I have apparently heard persons talking who were far away from me and/or perhaps read the thoughts of persons who were far away from me. I was too far away to hear them or to read their lips in my opinion. Also, on various occasions, others seem to have read my thoughts, based on their reactions.

The first occasion that I remember hearing a conversation from relatively far away was when I was a young boy in about the first grade on a trip with my dad, paternal grandfather, and a couple of other people. On a visit to a shipyard during that trip, a visit that only dad, my grandfather, and I took, I heard the voices of a couple talking; they were several feet away. My grandfather said to my dad that he heard those persons' voices through me and stated that "the boy has the hearing; maybe someone will teach him to talk when he gets older; maybe everyone can hear; maybe everyone can talk. We don't know much about how it works." My grandfather seemed to be referring to how people can hear voices from far away and speak in a voice that can be heard far away.

On some of the occasions that I hear these voices, if someone else is near me, sometimes the individual near me will touch one of their ears with a finger. Perhaps they are indicating they are hearing the same voice? Or, perhaps it is coincidence or a reaction to some mannerism of mine. The times I've asked, the person touching their ear didn't indicate hearing anything.

How does this super hearing or extra loud talking work? I feel it is a gift of God to be used for good.

Summary

God provides each of us with special gifts. My desire is to do God's perfect will—indeed, for all of us to do God's perfect will. Are some (or all) of us gifted with some form of special hearing ability and speech that conveys long distances under certain circumstances? Do our eyes have special powers that can be developed and used for exceptionally good purposes? If I am blessed with a gift of God, I desire to use it properly for good.

I feel I have experienced an unusually high number of events that are difficult to explain. Perhaps, though, many persons (or maybe all of us) experience at least some of these very unusual events. I don't know if I or anyone will ever completely understand them.

The closer we get to total devotion to God and God's perfect righteous will, the better the outcome of these occasions will be, as I see it. I pray for God's perfect will in all things.

Lots of other unusual things have happened to me, and I may write more about them, too, if I feel God desires me to. My desire is to write according to God's timetable, in a positive way that does good, in the way God desires, which requires God's leadership.

Just as I have experienced or observed several unusual events, I've gotten the opportunity to learn about some unusual places. In the next chapter I discuss one of them, a huge cave along the Kentucky-Virginia border that may be the world's second longest cave.

Chapter 49 Questions for Reflection and Discussion
1. Have you experienced highly unusual events in your life similar to any of those discussed in this chapter? If so, what?
2. Do you believe all the incidents described in this chapter are true? If not, how do you account for the author's memories of them? If you do believe them, do you have explanations for them?
3. Do you think it is appropriate to disclose such unusual events, or do you think many of them need to remain secret? What criteria would you use to decide which to disclose and when?

Chapter 50:
God's Magnificent Creation—Huge Cave Along the Kentucky-Virginia Border

True Christianity includes trying to appreciate and to care responsibly for God's magnificent creations. I feel that it is very important for humans to help preserve the wonderful planet God has provided. It would be a shame if wonders like the Grand Canyon, Great Smoky Mountains, Yellowstone, Yosemite, or other priceless natural treasures were irreparably damaged or destroyed.

The awesome diversity of our planet is an astounding testament to God, as I see it. Plants, animals, mountains, valleys, lakes, rivers, oceans, deserts, caves, etc., illustrate that. For the last topic in my book, I want to discuss one of those features, a magnificent cave in Kentucky—and not the one you are probably thinking about.

Here in Kentucky, numerous beautiful caves are one of the unusual features that add magnificent diversity to the area. Mammoth Cave is the best known one, famous for its spectacular beauty and for being the longest known cavern in the world. But among Kentucky's many caves is a second huge cave along the Kentucky-Virginia border. By the way, since the cavern is along the border between the two states, I'm not sure how much of it is in Kentucky and how much is in Virginia.

Huge Cave Along the Kentucky-Virginia Border

Telling about this cave may have little to do with Christianity directly, but I think the cave helps indicate the awesome beauty and diversity of God's creation. The cavern currently gets little attention, although it could be the second longest cave in the world. And its fabulous beauty may rival that of Mammoth Cave.

I'll preface my comments about it by urging readers not to rush down to see it due to the danger (as well as the risk of doing priceless damage to parts of the cavern and/or bats living in it). If you choose to visit anyway, please get permission from property owners, make sure you are well trained and equipped properly, tell a friend exactly where you are entering and when you will be exiting, and be very cautious. Caving can be extremely dangerous due to slippery surfaces, sudden drop-offs, overhanging rocks, flash flooding from unexpected rainfalls, and of course the risk of getting lost in a huge cave with numerous passages, in addition to other factors, including lack of oxygen in some cases. Please prepare carefully and thoroughly. Be aware also of federal and state laws that exist to protect caves and artifacts inside them.

By the way, this chapter is adapted from an article I wrote partially as a tribute to my dad, who enjoyed caving; that article was published on Yahoo! Voices, part of Yahoo! that has since been closed down by Yahoo!

Dad enjoyed reading the article about two months before he passed on to heaven (at age 82) on April 27, 2013. I told him I planned to include a chapter in my book about the cave.

Personally, I only went caving a few times with dad because of the dangers involved. I haven't been in a southeastern Kentucky cave in decades. But if/when parts of this huge cave are accessible for public tours, I would love to take a tour and see the river and some other marvelous sights I haven't seen personally—if I am still alive and fit enough to do so at that time. However, I urge readers desiring to tour a huge Kentucky cave soon to take one or more of the scheduled tours of Mammoth Cave in western Kentucky instead of entering this one. By the way, just as only a small part of Mammoth Cave is open to tours, at most I think only a small part of this huge cave along the Kentucky-Virginia border will ever be a public tourist attraction.

Explorations by the Author's Dad

This author's dad, William E. "Bill" Gibson, over a few decades explored parts of the cavern in his spare time. Dad told of its magnificent beauty to me and many others numerous times over the years, before he passed on to heaven. He described various beautiful colors, huge rooms, stalactites and stalagmites—and a river flowing through one level of it.

I think dad's explorations began as a search for silver mines allegedly operated by John Swift in the 18th century in Kentucky. But dad also enjoyed being outdoors, hiking, and caving. Though he never found a silver mine, dad said he did find some silver coins.

Dad called the cave "The Cavern of the Shawnees," which are words (or similar to words) that John Swift allegedly used, too, to describe it. Dad said several times that it extends at least from the Breaks area near Elkhorn City, Kentucky to the Cumberland Gap and Middlesboro area. This is a distance of more than 75 miles. And in one phone conversation he told me that it may begin before the Breaks and end past Middlesboro.

Dad told me the cave contains passages on multiple vertical levels. He added that numerous entrances lead into the cave.

If all the passages are mapped, this author believes that the total length of them could be a couple hundred miles, making it the world's second longest known cave.

Shawnee Indian Knowledge of the Cave

Though it lacks fame today, the cave apparently was well known centuries ago. The Shawnee Indians knew about the cave, according to the five volume 1922 *History of Kentucky*. The book states that Charles Blue-Jacket described the cave as "many miles in extent," stating "that it could be entered at several different points and on both sides of the great mountain range." The book also notes that "To the hoof-beats of the horse along the roadway through Pound Gap the mountain sounds . . . hollow, especially when the solid rock is trodden." (The five volume book that I quoted from in this paragraph was edited by Judge Charles Kerr, copyright 1922 by The American Historical Society, and discusses the cave on pages 128 and 129 of Volume I, in a chapter written by William Elsey Connelley.)

My dad told me multiple times that one part of the cave is very sacred to the Shawnee Indians. Dad said either that he was told or that he read (I'm not sure which) "that no white man will ever enter" that part of the cave. That may be true. And I think it is very important to try to take reasonable steps to protect the entire cave from abuse and damage.

Explorations by Ray Love

Ray Love, after exploring parts of the cave in 1971, provided an awesome description, reported by Kenneth Paul Mink in the Hazard, Kentucky *Hazard Herald* newspaper in its April 30, 1971 issue. Numerous other news sources carried this impressive report via the Associated Press. In May 1971 various publications provided more details about the cave, Ray Love's explorations, and the cave potentially becoming a major tourist attraction for the area.

Recent Years and the Future

As far as I know, the media has written little about the cave in recent decades. It certainly has not become a major tourist attraction.

Furthermore, I am concerned that damage possibly occurred to parts of the cave during construction of a four-lane road some years ago over the mountain between Jenkins, Kentucky and Virginia. Also, quarrying operations in various locations along the many miles of the area where the cave exists potentially can damage it—if they haven't already. Additionally, irresponsible spelunkers may damage it and steal items for their personal collections, as some probably have.

Much of the cave is on private property. This can be good or bad depending on how property owners care for it.

Somehow the cave needs protected from those who would abuse it. Also, keeping numerous cave entrances open is important for ventilation and for easy access to the lengthy cave. Unfortunately, several entrances have already been sealed.

The ongoing formation of the Pine Mountain State Scenic Trail, a linear state park that basically follows the area of the cave, may help protect this underground marvel. But that remains to be seen.

Cave Is a Priceless Treasure of Unknown Size

This cave seems to be a priceless treasure. Its natural beauty is one reason, but items possibly left in it by Indians, early settlers, etc., may make it even more magnificent. Perhaps ancient peoples that preceded the Indians explored the cave and left priceless artifacts. It would be a terrible shame if vandals damaged or destroyed either these items or the cave itself, or if artifacts were permanently lost due to entrances being sealed up—as many entrances already have been.

Only God knows the total size of the cavern, and I doubt that any human has explored more than a small part of it. Reasons for this include limitations on the length of time lights last, as well as the need to carry adequate rope, food, and other items underground. Also, many of the entrances are small, which discourages some explorers.

Descriptions provided by my dad, Ray Love, Blue-Jacket, and others indicate the cave is a magnificent wonder of nature. It would be marvelous if more actions are taken to preserve this priceless treasure for future generations. Perhaps at least parts of it can be developed as a tourist attraction, too.

Let's seek to protect this priceless underground marvel and all the other priceless creations God has provided, when reasonably possible. I consider this part of practicing "True Christianity."

In this book I've covered a wide variety of topics related to my concept of true Christianity. In the next chapter, the final one, I provide a short summary/epilogue.

Chapter 50 Questions for Reflection and Discussion

1. What do you think should be done to preserve the cave?

2. What steps would you advocate taking to preserve natural wonders in your area?
3. Does seeing wonders of nature like the cave described in this chapter (or Mammoth Cave or the Grand Canyon, etc.) help you appreciate the existence of a greater power than humans that creates and controls the way things work?

This chapter concludes Part IV. But before moving on to part V, please take time to briefly review Part IV. The questions below may help.
1. How do you feel Christianity relates to other religions?
2. Is agnosticism a more realistic belief than atheism?
3. Do kabbalah, hypnotism, and ESP have a place in Christianity?
4. What other important issue(s) do you feel could have been included in this part? What issue(s) (if any) would you have omitted?

Part V: Summary

Chapter 51:
Summary/Epilogue

True Christianity has been defined over the centuries by a lot of people in many different ways. In this book I sought to provide my own definition of it, as well as to write about specific attitudes, beliefs, and behaviors that I consider aspects of practicing true Christianity. After doing this, in Part IV I discussed how I felt Christianity related to several other beliefs, actions, and facts; I concluded by discussing several unusual events and a cave that is a wonder of nature.

My hope is that what I've written here helps readers come closer to being "true Christians," being perfectly obedient to God, the highest righteous authority, loving others and yourselves.

I desire for God's perfect will to be done in all things. I feel we are all blessed by God in numerous ways. If we seek to appreciate these blessings and to use our gifts to better ourselves and others, we can make our world a much better place.

I'll repeat some words I stated back in the first chapter in the next two paragraphs:

"Some persons refer to Christians as being 'born again.' This term is accurate in the sense that instead of continuing to live their lives selfishly according to their natural desires, after becoming Christians persons commit to obeying the highest righteous authority, God, and thus commit to seeking what is best: showing love to others and to themselves.

"Doing this is somewhat like living a new life. I urge readers to seek to do this. Confess your sins, renounce them, and prayerfully seek to be obedient to God, loving others and yourselves. In simple terms, obeying the highest righteous authority (which I call God) by loving and caring for others and oneself is what true Christianity is all about. Using this definition, even those who do not profess to be Christians can seek to practice true Christianity."

I don't urge everyone to literally follow the radical approach to Christianity that Jesus advocated in Mark 10:21, when he instructed a rich man to sell everything and follow him. But for some readers who are relatively wealthy, selling much and devoting more time and energy to ministering to others may be part of their calling. Traveling more, learning another language, and serving as a short-term or career missionary may be part of their calling.

Living with fewer possessions can be a blessing. Personally, I enjoy living in a studio efficiency apartment and renting a car periodically instead of owning a house and car, partly for economic reasons. But I'm not advocating that for everyone, either.

Also, please note that despite the breadth of this book, many topics were omitted. Furthermore, remember that numerous subjects covered received only brief mention. Still, thanks to God, I am confident that readers who prayerfully read the entire book benefitted significantly from their reading.

My goal is to write as God desires, to make a positive impact, to make things better. The book title, *True Christianity: It May Not Be What You Think*, is I think very appropriate. But it is also true that true Christianity may not be what I think it is either. I certainly don't have perfect insight into God.

My email address is given on the copyright page and repeated in the introduction so persons can contact me. I trust that with constructive criticism from readers, this Third Edition of the book can be revised sometime into an even better Fourth Edition, God willing. I also hope to write on other matters as well, God willing.

This book doesn't discuss every virtue of a true Christian or every vice of those who are not true Christians. But I think reading it can make an excellent starting point on the right path for many.

Wouldn't it be great to see everyone practicing true Christianity? It would be wonderful to see more people:

- picking up litter off the ground—fewer throwing it down.
- speaking kind words—fewer cursing.
- donating money to charity—fewer spending money on tattoos, piercings, or tans.
- buying quality food—fewer buying tobacco, beer, lottery tickets, and junk food.
- thinking positively—fewer complaining.
- loving family and friends—fewer lying, stealing, and fighting.
- helping those different from themselves—fewer criticizing them.
- practicing sexual abstinence—fewer aborting unborn children.
- seeking to practice true Christianity—fewer seeking selfish gain.

I realize some will feel that I am too liberal in stating that persons not professing to be Christians (and not having been baptized) can be true Christians. But who knows? A November 2013 Associated Press article (http://www.usatoday.com/story/news/nation/2013/11/10/atheist-mega-churches/3489967/)[33] discusses "atheist mega-churches" that feature many of the elements of traditional churches.

Just as some will think I am too liberal, I realize some will feel I am too conservative on tattoos, piercings, and various other issues; they may feel that I am harping on minor things. Just as Jesus suffered from criticism from various sources (and received praise from others), true Christians will too, in my view.

For readers who desire to focus on improving in specific areas covered in certain chapters in this book, I urge them to reread those portions prayerfully, then write down a specific list of things they desire to change, as well as steps to take to implement the changes. Pray over the list each morning as part of a morning devotional time and each evening as part of an evening devotional time; do this daily for at least six weeks, and I am confident you will experience positive changes in your lives.

Thanks for reading! Enjoy God's blessings!

Chapter 51 Questions for Reflection and Discussion
1. Did the book change your view about true Christianity? If so, how?
2. Do you think this book oversimplifies some things? If so, list examples. Do you think this book makes some things too complex? If so, list examples. Do you think the book does well overall in covering the basic principles of practicing true Christianity?

Endnotes (Details for Internet Links in the Book)

Webpages and websites frequently change location or cease to exist. I hope the information in these Endnotes helps readers locate articles, even if the webpages are relocated or no longer exist. All webpages whose URLs are in the book (from the Introduction through the Summary) are listed, in chronological order.

For each reference, I list the date I accessed the webpage. In cases where I list the last date the webpage was updated, that is as of the date I accessed the webpage; the webpage may have been updated since the day I accessed it. I checked all the links in May 2019 (and previously in September 2017 and August 2015) to determine whether or not that they still worked. I found that in some cases the material had been updated. In a few cases the titles of the pieces, etc., were changed slightly. However, I stuck with my original citation information, except as noted in the following Endnotes. In cases where the original link actually now connected to another similar URL, I also listed the alternative URL. If the original link was inactive, I added an active link.

The Internet is a great resource. Unfortunately, unlike hard copies that may remain in a library for centuries, online versions may disappear if the website closes down. I hope hard copies continue to exist for much (if not all) important information.

[1] Charles Choi; "Wooly Mammoths Could Be Cloned Someday, Scientist Says"; LiveScience.com; December 8, 2011; website accessed April 8, 2012.
http://www.livescience.com/17386-woolly-mammoth-clone.html

[2] Innocence Project; website accessed May 24, 2019; https://www.innocenceproject.org

[3] "Death Penalty and Innocence"; Amnesty International USA; website accessed September 2, 2017.
https://www.amnestyusa.org/issues/death-penalty/death-penalty-facts/death-penalty-and-innocence/

[4] "Facts About the Death Penalty"; The Death Penalty Information Center (Updated September 28, 2010); website accessed September 28, 2010.
http://www.deathpenaltyinfo.org/documents/FactSheet.pdf

[5] Jennifer Viegas; "How sex with Neanderthals made us stronger"; Discovery News, posted on NBCNews.com; updated August 25, 2011; website accessed September 2, 2017.
http://www.nbcnews.com/id/44277901/ns/technology_and_science-science/t/how-sex-neanderthals-made-us-stronger/#.War6vch97IU (In May 2019 the link still worked but connected to the URL following the colon: http:www.nbcnews.com/id/44277901/ns/technology_and_science-science/t/how-sex-neanderthals-made-us-stronger/#.XOWm7uTsblW)

[6] "Dietary Health"; United States Department of Agriculture; (Last Date Modified, June 19, 2013); website accessed June 21, 2013.
http://www.usda.gov/wps/portal/usda/usdahome?navid=DIETARY_HEALTH&navtype=RT&parentnav=FOOD_NUTRITION
(On September 1, 2017 the link still worked but connected to the webpage following the colon: https://www.usda.gov/topics/food-and-nutrition/dietary-health)

[7] Betty Kovacs (Medical Editor, Melissa Conrad Stoppler); "Vegetarian and Vegan Diet"; MedicineNet.com; (The link I provide in my book is directly to page two of the article, a section subtitled "What are the potential health problems from consuming a vegetarian and vegan diet?"); website accessed August 30, 2009.

http://www.medicinenet.com/vegetarian_and_vegan_diet/page2.htm
(On September 1, 2017 the link still worked but connected to the webpage that follows the colon: http://www.medicinenet.com/vegetarian_and_vegan_diet/article.htm)

[8] "Sexually transmitted infections (STI) Fact Sheet." Womenshealth.gov. U.S. Department of Health and Human Services. Last updated November 16, 2009; website accessed December 9, 2012.
http://womenshealth.gov/publications/our-publications/fact-sheet/sexually-transmitted-infections.cfm
(The link still worked on August 15, 2014, but it connected to the webpage following the colon: http://womenshealth.gov/publications/our-publications/fact-sheet/sexually-transmitted-infections.html)
(The second link still worked on September 1, 2017, but it connected to the webpage that follows the colon: https://www.womenshealth.gov/a-z-topics/sexually-transmitted-infections) The webpage connected to in the link accessed on September 1, 2017 was updated in 2017, but it contains similar information to the one I accessed in 2012. The quote in the text of this book is from the source I accessed in 2012.

[9] Bill Albert; "With One Voice 2012: America's Adults and Teens Sound Off About Teen Pregnancy: A Periodic National Survey." The National Campaign to Prevent Teen and Unplanned Pregnancy. August 2012. (Based on telephone surveys conducted by Social Science Research Solutions in March and April 2012.); website accessed on September 3, 2017.
https://thenationalcampaign.org/sites/default/files/resource-primary-download/wov_2012.pdf

(In May 2019 the link did not work, but I accessed the document at the website following the colon: https://success1st.org/uploads/3/4/5/1/34510348/wov_2012.pdf)

[10] Danice K. Eaton, Laura Kann, Steve Kinchen, Shari Shanklin, Katherine H. Flint, Joseph Hawkins, William A. Harris, Richard Lowry, Tim McManus, David Chyen, Lisa Whittle, Connie Lim, Howell Wechsler; "Youth Risk Behavior Surveillance—United States, 2011"; Centers for Disease Control and Prevention. Morbidity and Mortality Weekly Report. Surveillance Summaries, June 8, 2012, Vol. 61, #SS-4; website accessed December 9, 2012. http://www.cdc.gov/mmwr/preview/mmwrhtml/ss6104a1.htm

[11] Edmonds, Molly; "Does living together before marriage lead to divorce?" Discovery Health. Howstuffworks.com; Discovery Communications, Inc.; website accessed on September 17, 2013. http://health.howstuffworks.com/relationships/advice/living-together-before-marriage.htm

[12] "Alcohol and Public Health: Frequently Asked Questions"; Centers for Disease Control and Prevention. Last updated July 31, 2013; website accessed on September 17, 2013.
http://www.cdc.gov/alcohol/faqs.htm
(On September 1, 2017 the link still worked, but the webpage was updated in 2017. My quote in the text of the book is from the original access to the website in 2013.)

[13] Alcohol Alert. National Institute on Alcohol Abuse and Alcoholism. No. 52; April 2001. Posted June 2001; website accessed on August 21, 2010.
http://pubs.niaaa.nih.gov/publications/aa52.htm

[14] "Alcohol & Cardiovascular Disease"; American Heart Association; website accessed on September 17, 2013.

http://www.heart.org/HEARTORG/Conditions/More/MyHeartandStrokeNews/Alcohol-and-Heart-Disease_UCM_305173_Article.jsp

(On September 1, 2017 the link still worked but connected to the webpage following the colon: http://www.heart.org/HEARTORG/Conditions/More/MyHeartandStrokeNews/Alcohol-and-Heart-Disease_UCM_305173_Article.jsp#.Wamrpsh97IU) The quote used in this book from the webpage accessed in 2013 is on the webpage accessed September 1, 2017, too.

(In May 2019 both the above links still worked. But, both connected to the webpage following the colon: https://www.heart.org/en/healthy-living/eating/eat-smart/nutrition-basics/alcohol-and-heart-health)

[15] Martha Grogan; Answer to question, "Does grape juice offer the same heart benefits as red wine?"; MayoClinic.com, July 23, 2011; website accessed on September 17, 2013.

http://www.mayoclinic.com/health/food-and-nutrition/AN00576

(The link still worked on March 17, 2014, but it connected to the webpage following the colon: http://www.mayoclinic.org/healthy-living/nutrition-and-healthy-eating/expert-answers/food-and-nutrion/faq-20058529)

(On September 1, 2017 the second link still worked, but it connected to the webpage following the colon: http://www.mayoclinic.org/healthy-lifestyle/nutrition-and-healthy-eating/expert-answers/food-and-nutrition/faq-20058529) The new webpage cites Katherine Zeratsy as a source, but the information is similar to what Martha Grogan provided on the webpage accessed in 2013 for the reference in the text of this book.

[16] Roni Caryn Rabin; "Alcohol's Good for You? Some Scientists Doubt It"; *New York Times* website, June 16, 2009; website accessed on August 21, 2010.

http://query.nytimes.com/gst/fullpage.html?res=9D05EFD81F3BF935A25755C0A96F9C8B63&sec=&spon=&pagewanted=1
(In May 2019 the link still worked but connected to the webpage following the colon: https://www.nytimes.com/2009/06/16/health/16alco.html)

[17] "H-30.940 AMA Policy Consolidation: Labeling Advertising and Promotion of Alcoholic Beverages"; American Medical Association website; website accessed on August 26, 2015.
https://www.ama-assn.org/ssl3/ecomm/PolicyFinderForm.pl?site=www.ama-assn.org&uri=/resources/html/PolicyFinder/policyfiles/HnE/H-30.940.HTM
(On September 2, 2017 this link did not work, but the document I quoted from could be found on the webpage following the colon: http://studylib.net/doc/8661926/health-and-ethics-policies---american-medical-association)

[18] "Alcohol and Public Health: Frequently Asked Questions"; Centers for Disease Control and Prevention. Last updated July 31, 2013; website accessed on September 17, 2013.
http://www.cdc.gov/alcohol/faqs.htm

[19] "Alcohol and Global Health: Executive Summary"; TheLancet.com. Published June 26, 2009; website accessed on August 21, 2010.
http://www.thelancet.com/series/alcohol-and-global-health

[20] "Worldwide Blood Alcohol Concentration (BAC) Limits"; DrinkDriving.org website; website accessed August 26, 2015.
http://www.drinkdriving.org/worldwide_drink_driving_limits.php

[21] "DietaryGuidelines.gov: Dietary Guidelines for Americans"; Health.gov; website accessed June 23, 2013.

http://www.health.gov/dietaryguidelines/

[22] United States Department of Agriculture; ChooseMyPlate.gov; website accessed April 20, 2012.
http://www.choosemyplate.gov/

[23] Andrea Carlson, Mark Lino, WenYen Juan, Kenneth Hanson, and P. Peter Basiotis; "Thrifty Food Plan, 2006"; Center for Nutrition Policy and Promotion, United States Department of Agriculture, CNPP-19; April 2007; website accessed August 26, 2015.
http://www.cnpp.usda.gov/sites/default/files/usda_food_plans_cost_of_food/TFP2006Report.pdf
(In May 2019 the link did not go directly to the document, but the document could be downloaded from a link on the webpage following the colon: https://ideas.repec.org/p/ags/usacnr/42899.html)

[24] Center for Nutrition Policy and Promotion, United States Department of Agriculture; "Official USDA Food Plans: Cost of Food at Home at Four Levels, U.S. Average, April 2019"; Center for Nutrition Policy and Promotion, United States Department of Agriculture; Issued May 2019; website accessed May 24, 2019.
https://fns-prod.azureedge.net/sites/default/files/resource-files/CostofFoodApr2019.pdf

[25] FEMA.gov; "Emergency Supplies List"; FEMA.gov; website accessed September 2, 2017.
https://www.fema.gov/media-library-data/1e04d512b273e2133cb865833cc0e32d/FEMA_checklist_parent_508_071513.pdf

[26] Ready.gov; Ready.gov website homepage; Ready.gov; website accessed September 2, 2017.

https://www.ready.gov/

[27] American Red Cross; "Safe Generator Use"; American Red Cross website; website accessed August 26, 2015.
http://www.redcross.org/prepare/disaster/power-outage/safe-generator-use
(On September 2, 2017 the link still worked, but it connected to the webpage following the colon: http://www.redcross.org/get-help/how-to-prepare-for-emergencies/types-of-emergencies/power-outage/safe-generator-use#What-size-generator-will-I-need-)
(In May 2019 both links still worked, but they connected to the webpage following the colon: https://www.redcross.org/get-help/how-to-prepare-for-emergencies/types-of-emergencies/power-outage/safe-generator-use.html)

[28] "Prom Health and Safety Tips"; Centers for Disease Control and Prevention (Last modified March 26, 2012); website accessed January 15, 2013.
http://www.cdc.gov/family/prom/

[29] Carleton Kendrick; "Prom Safety"; FamilyEducation.com; website accessed January 15, 2013.
http://life.familyeducation.com/teen/prom/36549.html
(On September 2, 2017 the link still worked, but it connected to the webpage following the colon: https://www.familyeducation.com/life/prom/prom-safety)

[30] "Project MKULTRA, The CIA's Program of Research in Behavioral Modification"; Joint Hearing Before the Select Committee on Intelligence and the Subcommittee on Health and Scientific Research of the Committee on Human Resources: United States Senate, Ninety Fifth Congress, First Session, August 3, 1977; accessed on website of *New York Times*; website accessed March 11, 2014.

https://www.nytimes.com/packages/pdf/national/13inmate_Project MKULTRA.pdf

[31] Elaine Woo; "CIA's Gottlieb Ran LSD Mind Control Testing"; LATimes.com; April 4, 1999; website accessed March 11, 2014.
http://articles.latimes.com/1999/apr/04/local/me-24126
(In May 2019 the link still worked but connected to the webpage following the colon: https://www.latimes.com/archieves/la-xpm-1999-apr-04-me-24126-story.html)

[32] Nate Rawlings; "CIA Mind-Control Experiments"; Time.com; August 6, 2010; (Part of a Time.com piece titled "Top 10 Weird Government Secrets"); website accessed March 11, 2014.
http://content.time.com/time/specials/packages/article/0,28804,2008962_2008964_2008992,00.html

[33] Associated Press; "Atheist mega-churches look for nonbelievers"; Associated Press; accessed on website of USAToday.com; November 10, 2013; website accessed November 12, 2013.
http://www.usatoday.com/story/news/nation/2013/11/10/atheist-mega-churches/3489967/

About the Author

James E. Gibson is a former agnostic who became a Christian during his college years. He has written a second book, *Several True (I Think) Stories: Can Truth Be Stranger Than Fiction?* (2016, second edition 2017). About 35-40% of its stories are reprinted or adapted from stories printed in *True Christianity*. He has also written numerous articles for websites such as Google Blogger, Yahoo! Voices (and its predecessor Associated Content), Newsvine, and Helium.

Though the author is a Christian layperson, not a Bible scholar, he has read the Bible in English a few times and devoted several hours to reading in two local seminaries. The author is a graduate of the University of Kentucky. His undergraduate electives included several English courses and his graduate school coursework included some Communications courses.

He holds B.S. degrees in mining engineering and civil engineering, as well as an MBA. Since his childhood he has loved to read and write. As a bivocational freelance writer, he has worked a variety of second jobs to help keep the bills paid while seeking to fulfill his dream of developing a writing career.

A series of unusual events/coincidences and the author's inappropriate way of speaking about them led to a series of things that resulted in a few brief psychiatric hospitalizations for him and outpatient psychiatric treatment during the period of 1993 to 1996. But he was blessed immeasurably during that time and is blessed immeasurably now as well. That period gave him additional insights into Christianity.

The author is a very ecumenical nondenominational Christian who is not currently a formal member of any specific Christian congregation though he enjoys visiting various churches (and has even visited a mosque and a synagogue). He feels there are nice persons in each congregation and feels linked to each as part of the worldwide Christian church.

He would love for everyone to live happier, healthier, longer, more fulfilling lives with no sin, pain, or suffering and then go on to live forever in heaven. He feels that as we come closer to practicing true Christianity, we come closer to reaching this ideal, too.

Order Form and Ordering Information

If you would like an additional copy (or copies) of this book, you can order or buy it (or them) from a bookstore, Amazon.com, and other sources. You may also use the order form at the bottom of this page to order one copy shipped to a location in the 48 contiguous states of the United States (not Alaska or Hawaii).

On all orders please add $4 for shipping and handling.
Kentucky residents please add 6% state sales tax to the total cost.

Sorry, no returns allowed. Prices subject to change without notice. Payment accepted by check or money order. Please allow 30 days for delivery. Thanks! Books will be shipped directly from the printer.

If you desire to order two or more copies, please email me at jamesegibson@gmail.com for prices and terms, or write me at the Post Office Box address below. If you write my Post Office Box address, please enclose a self-addressed, stamped envelope. Thanks!

Also, you may email or write for prices and terms to buy a copy of the second edition of my second book, *Several True (I Think) Stories: Can Truth Be Stranger Than Fiction?* About 35-40% of the stories in this second book are reprinted or adapted from stories in *True Christianity: It May Not Be What You Think*.

Please send me one copy of the third edition of *True Christianity: It May Not Be What You Think* for a price of $14 + $4 for shipping and handling + $1.08 for Kentucky state sales tax if being mailed to a Kentucky address (omit the $1.08 if your mailing address is outside of Kentucky).

Here is my check or money order for $19.08 (or $18.00 if your mailing address is outside of Kentucky). Orders accepted for the 48 contiguous states of the United States only (excludes Alaska and Hawaii).

Name...
Address..
City/State...
Zip Code...
Email Address (optional)............................

Please make your check or money order out to James E. Gibson. Mail orders to: James E. Gibson, P.O. Box 54868, Lexington, KY 40555-4868

---

www.ingramcontent.com/pod-product-compliance
Lightning Source LLC
Chambersburg PA
CBHW070602300426
44113CB00010B/1371